GEORGE BEST

GEORGE BEST

The Extraordinary Story of a Footballing Genius

BY IVAN PONTING

SIMON &
SCHUSTER

London · New York · Sydney · Toronto · New Delhi

A CBS COMPANY

First published in Great Britain by
Simon & Schuster UK Ltd, 2012
A CBS COMPANY

Simon & Schuster UK Ltd
1st Floor
222 Gray's Inn Road
London
WC1X 8HB

www.simonandschuster.co.uk

Simon & Schuster Australia, Sydney
Simon & Schuster India, New Delhi

A CIP catalogue record for this book is available
from the British Library

ISBN: 978-1-84983-807-8

Designed and typeset by Nick Venables

Printed and bound by FIRMENGRUPPE APPL,
aprinta druck, Wemding, Germany

GEORGE BEST
CONTENTS

FOREWORD BY SIR BOBBY CHARLTON   1

FOREWORD BY DENIS LAW   4

INTRODUCTION   7

1   BAG OF BONES WITH A GOLDEN GIFT   12

2   ON THE THRESHOLD OF SOMETHING REMARKABLE   22

3   'YOU'RE IN TODAY, SON'   34

4   WONDER BOY   50

5   'EL BEATLE' SHREDS THE SCRIPT   68

6   BACK TO THE PINNACLE   82

7   GOALSCORER-IN-CHIEF   100

8   LIVING THE ULTIMATE DREAM   116

9   ANXIOUS TIMES   134

10   A TURNAROUND – BUT IT'S ONLY TEMPORARY   152

11   ON THE SLIPPERY SLOPE   168

12   A SEISMIC CONVULSION   184

13   BREAKING POINT   200

14   THE PRIDE AND THE FRUSTRATION   210

15   WHEN BESTIE MET PELÉ   226

16   IN BRONZE FOR ETERNITY   240

ACKNOWLEDGEMENTS   249

PICTURE CREDITS   250

FOREWORD BY SIR BOBBY CHARLTON

I don't recall anything about George Best's first game for Manchester United, but his second, against Burnley in December 1963, is ingrained in my mind. It was the second part of one of those Christmas double-headers that we used to play, and Matt Busby was shaking up the team because two days earlier we had been hammered 6–1 at Turf Moor. So in came George on the left wing and he was pitted against a good pal of mine, the Clarets' right-back, John Angus. Now John was a fine player, talented enough to have earned an England cap only two seasons earlier, and he might have collected many more had he not been unfortunate enough to perform in an era when first Jimmy Armfield and then George Cohen laid unassailable claim to their country's number two shirt.

That day, though, my mate looked anything but a world-beater as the 17-year-old George tormented him, really took him to the cleaners. I'd heard from our coaches that the wispy little fellow from Belfast was going to be a bit special, and now I found out exactly what they meant. All the gifts that we came to know and marvel at were on show – the speed, the balance, the close control and the nerve to put all the attributes together on the big stage of Old Trafford in front of a holiday crowd disgruntled by our comprehensive defeat a couple of days earlier. We won the game 5–1, with George scoring once and helping to set up most of the others. After that, there was never the slightest doubt that he was going to the very top.

People still talk of him as if he was playing today. He is part of their lives and to them he was footballing perfection. Of course, nobody is that, but there were times when he did come close. He could do the unbelievable so often that you came to expect it. On the other hand, there were times when I wanted to scream at him for not passing the ball to me. One occasion that stands out was against Nottingham Forest, when he made me feel ridiculous in front of the Stretford End. So maddening could he be that I had promised myself that one day, when the game was safe and he expected me to run into space so that he could bounce the ball off me or even use me as a dummy, I simply wouldn't do it for him. In this game he ran right across the width of the pitch and back again with the little full-back Joe Wilson chasing him as if his life depended on it. I was blazing mad, utterly furious, and I made up my mind to stand still. Then, as he came close to me with the ball on his right foot, I started to moan: 'George, you greedy little . . . what a fantastic goal!' And that summed him up for me. He was a wonder of the footballing world.

One very personal memory of George is of an evening we spent together at a time when he was already recognised as one of the finest footballers on the planet. We had played together in a UEFA representative match at Ninian Park and caught the train back to Manchester from Cardiff.

At that point I was very much a family man, while George was invariably out on the town, living it up for all he was worth. Though we played for the same football club, our lives could hardly have been more different, but as the train headed north we were having a nice, friendly chat and I asked him what he had planned for later in the evening. He had nothing special lined up and so, knowing my wife and two daughters were away for the night, I asked him if he fancied coming back to my house for supper. Not that I'm a great chef, you understand, but Norma had told me there was a bag of frozen scampi in the fridge and I thought I could deal with that.

Though I meant the invitation sincerely, I didn't dream he would accept, but he did, and we passed a lovely few hours together. George surprised me by being full of questions about my life of domesticity, being married, running the house, having a dog. I got the impression that he was toying with the idea of settling down himself, perhaps wanting a little bit of peace instead of being constantly in the glare of publicity.

I think he revealed something of himself that I had never seen before. He was friendly and fully engaged, and perhaps a tiny bit insecure beneath the aura of glitz and glamour that had become so much part of his way of life. It was as though he was looking for something a bit more solid, something that was more real, and which might lead in the longer term to less intrusive probing by the media. Eventually I drove him into town and when I dropped him off I was left to reflect on a rather strange but enlightening evening. I hope he enjoyed it, too.

Of course, everyone knows that George and I had a few differences about the way a professional footballer should live his life, for the good of both himself and his club, but I think the situation between us tended to be exaggerated. Happily, in later years we put

any difficulties behind us and our relationship had grown gratifyingly warm long before his death in 2005. That was right and fitting because, after all, we had shared so much that was uplifting in our time together at Old Trafford.

From this distance, when I picture George in my mind's eye, I can still feel the enchantment of his beautiful and natural talent. I see him selling dummies, running defenders ragged, scoring seemingly impossible goals, and continuing to turn on his magic in the face of relentless physical punishment. Sometimes he hit the deck, of course, but he managed to stay upright when subjected to the most ferocious treatment imaginable. Everyone recalls the goal he scored against Chelsea in the League Cup in 1970, when a defender tried to hack him down but he just kept running with the ball until he went round Peter Bonetti and scored.

Eventually you could see that he was beginning to lose some of that scintillating edge that set him apart from just about every other player in the land. It did grieve me when he stepped aside from United at the age of only 27 because it's not often that you get truly great players, and so it's tragic, in a sporting sense, if they don't fulfil their potential as a result of their lifestyle.

Having said all that, his fans couldn't have loved him any more than they did, something that never stopped for the rest of his life. To so many people George was the ultimate footballer; he brought to the game a true sense of wonder, exquisite moments of sheer joy, and for them there will never be anyone to match him. In the final analysis, I can only give thanks that I knew and played alongside George Best and, like everybody else, had been spellbound by the timeless glory of his unique gifts.

Sir Bobby Charlton, October 2012

FOREWORD BY DENIS LAW

The first time I laid eyes on George Best, on the training ground in the summer of 1962 following my arrival from Torino, he was 16 years old and just one of a posse of young hopefuls dreaming of a gilded future at Old Trafford. But long before he was called up by Matt Busby for his first-team debut in September 1963, it was blatantly obvious that he was on a different plane to the other kids, with no disrespect to them. There was always something special about the little fella from Belfast, a spark, some magical ingredient that was difficult to define but absolutely clear cut. I knew, the Boss knew, and pretty soon the world would discover that George Best was something else, a talent that didn't come along every day, nor even every decade – perhaps once or twice in a lifetime, if you were lucky.

So even though he was only 17 at the time, it was no great surprise to me when he was brought into the team for the visit of West Bromwich Albion. That day he was up against a decent and very tough full-back in Graham Williams who, as I recall, dumped our lad on the seat of his pants a time or two. But George just got up and got on with the game – and that's when I said to myself that he had a real chance of making the grade. Ability is important, of course it is, but attitude is vital, too, and this newcomer couldn't be faulted on either count.

It's a fact of football life that sometimes a player can be fabulous in training, absolutely dazzling, but when he runs out in front of 60,000 people on a Saturday afternoon, he just isn't the same performer. It's as though all the confidence drains away when he finds himself in the spotlight. But George, he just stepped into that massive arena and played as though he was training at The Cliff. He wasn't overawed in the slightest, nothing fazed him. Then when he returned for his second game, against Burnley just after Christmas in that same season, he did enough to convince us all that he was no flash in the pan, that he was a truly great player in the making.

Of course, nobody is perfect and, as a footballer, although he was one of the very finest the world has ever seen, there were times when he would infuriate you because he wouldn't give you the ball after you had busted a gut making a run for it. Jimmy Johnstone of Celtic and Scotland, another fabulously gifted winger and, I would say, one of the most magnificent talents of all time, could be like that, too. They were both wonderful people and I loved them dearly, but I must admit that their occasional disinclination to pass the ball could annoy you, make you feel just a little bit frustrated. True, quite often George stunned us by scoring fantastic goals out of nothing when we thought he should have parted with the ball but there were also times when he didn't score but might have passed to someone in a better position.

How did he handle his elevation to stardom on a personal level? I have no idea. I was six years older than him. I was married with children, and he was single. We just did our training, did our job and then went our separate ways. I was an old man to him in those days. It wasn't until long after we had retired that I became much closer to him as an individual, by which time the six-year age gap didn't make a scrap of difference.

What I *can* tell you is that, by nature, he was no Big-Time Charlie. The whole publicity thing was thrust upon him by the press. He was always a good lad, and a modest one, but it just so happened that his rise to worldwide prominence coincided with the beginning of showbiz razzmatazz entering the world of football. The Second World War was now well behind us, the Swinging Sixties were under way, and the media needed a figure like George. He was dubbed the fifth Beatle, and in the spring of 1966 his public profile was changed forever, after coming back from our 5–1 win over Benfica in Lisbon wearing his sombrero. After that, they never left him alone, not as long as he lived.

So much has been made of his lifestyle away from the game as the years went by that I don't need to comment on it, but I would like to say something about a widespread impression that has grown up, that George was somehow discontented with his teammates after United won the European Cup in 1968. It's been attributed to him that he was approaching his prime while many of us were content with what had been achieved, that we had lost our ambition and were ready for the knacker's yard. Rubbish! I was there at the time and I take serious issue with that suggestion. Bestie never gave the slightest indication to us or to Matt Busby that his teammates were letting him down or that they were past their best. Quite simply, he didn't have that way of thinking. Never in a million years. I believe the impression that he was unhappy with us was created by the media somewhere down the line. It was planted into his head, it was said over and over again so that it grew and grew, until eventually the myth became accepted as fact.

I don't deny that with the benefit of hindsight the team was not as good as it had been, that replacements were needed for one or two of the older players, that a couple of top-quality signings were needed to freshen things up. But don't forget that after winning the European Cup, we almost reached the final in the next season – and we would have, but for an appalling refereeing decision in the semi-final against AC Milan. So where's the lack of ambition there? Where's the lack of competitiveness?

In fact, I believe George was far more frustrated about having to play so many games with a debilitating knee injury. He was one of a group of us – including myself, Nobby Stiles and John Fitzpatrick – for whom the medical treatment on offer didn't turn out well. Injuries have an effect on the body, of course, but also on the personality and how you face everyday life. George was not helped by that, and I think that contributed massively to some of his difficulties.

The fact that he could still score 26 goals in a season, which he did as late as 1971/72, while nowhere near fully fit – and while not living like a monk, to put it mildly – makes me certain that, for all his achievements, we never saw the very best of George. After his cartilage operation was unsuccessful, he went on the blink at 26, exactly the age that a footballer should be approaching his peak years. Now it shouldn't be forgotten that he started young, and gave United a decade of deathless memories, but what might he have achieved if fully fit? The mind boggles.

As it was, he was one of the greatest footballers the game has ever seen, certainly among the top ten of my experience. Unhesitatingly I'd place him in the illustrious company of Di Stefano, Puskas, Pelé, Bobby, Eusebio, Greaves, Beckenbauer, Maradona and Cruyff. So on the whole, George Best didn't do too badly, did he? I feel proud and privileged that he was my teammate and, ultimately, my friend.

Denis Law, October 2012

INTRODUCTION

To many admirers of George Best, particularly those blessed enough to have watched him regularly during his pomp of nearly a decade, illuminating football fields the length and breadth of Europe with his incandescent talent, there is one abiding frustration. It is not that the Irish phenomenon gave short measure by leaving the elite echelons of the game at a time when his star should have been at its zenith. No, the vexation arises from the persistent notion that in some way he sold his public short.

Clearly, a few more years of his sublime genius would have been a golden gift, to an ailing Manchester United in particular and to the football world in general, but even a cursory examination of his record reveals that Best scaled dizzy heights and over a lengthier period than some of his most waspish critics allow. His tangible achievements include two League championships and an integral role in lifting the European Cup, a triumph that meant so much more to the Old Trafford institution than merely the gathering in of another trophy, no matter how gilded its status.

The true glory of Wembley 1968 represented the fulfilment of a quest that began a dozen seasons earlier, when Matt Busby and his Babes blazed a trail for English clubs in continental competition, in the face of small-minded opposition by the domestic authorities. Along the way United encountered the starkest of tragedy, suffering the devastation of the Munich air disaster, in which virtually a whole team of exquisitely gifted, compellingly potent young footballers lost their lives.

It was a calamity from which any club might never have recovered – but when it did, when Manchester United clawed its way to the very pinnacle of the club game, completing a uniquely emotional sporting journey by overcoming Portugal's mighty Benfica on that balmy, draining, unforgettable spring evening at the famous old arena, George Best was somehow the personification of all the collective excellence that had gone before.

Of course, he was supremely skilful with the ball at his feet, a veritable wizard. Mostly, too, he was intelligent in the application of his ability, even if occasionally he might drive his teammates to distraction as they waited in vain for a pass that never came. Physically, though slightly built, Best was brave beyond measure, routinely soaking up horrendous punishment from the mere mortals whose task it was to suppress his magic, and invariably bouncing back for more.

But beyond all that, he was daring, possessed of a devilish twinkle that communicated his natural joy at elevating the game to an irresistibly exciting level, and that was precisely the quality that rendered him the perfect heir to the perished Babes.

'Genius' is a term so chronically overused to describe sportsmen and women that it is in danger of being comprehensively devalued. It should be rationed scrupulously, reserved for the truly sublime rather than being squandered on the merely remarkable. However, there should be no hesitation in dusting down the word for a rare fitting recipient, and such a man was George Best.

Look beyond the lurid, fast-living image and set aside, for a moment, the alcoholism that was destined to transform his life so tragically – certainly, that is the approach adopted in this volume, which seeks to celebrate his extraordinary gifts rather than embark on cod-psychological analysis of his personal problems. They have been examined ad nauseam in the past and receive no more than passing reference in these pages.

Like Stanley Matthews before him, Best was the symbol of footballing excellence for a whole generation. There were other magnificent players, including Bobby Charlton and Denis Law, his fellow members of Manchester United's glorious trinity, but in the hearts and minds of the majority of 1960s and '70s match-goers, the mercurial Irishman was on a pedestal of his own.

As Matt Busby, his Old Trafford mentor, put it: 'George had more ways of beating a player than anyone I've ever seen. He was unique in his gifts.' Unfortunately, he was singular, too, in that he was the first 'pop star' footballer, whose every off-field action was scrutinised by the media. Relevant advice was scant, there being no precedent to his situation, and eventually the ceaseless attention, in which he revelled at first but subsequently reviled, goaded him inexorably towards self-destruction.

Despite that, despite everything, the game he illuminated so brilliantly remained his defining passion to the last. He was addicted to alcohol and he was addicted to women. But most of all he was addicted to football.

George left unanswerable questions behind him. How great might he have become but

for the bottle? Had Matt Busby been younger and in more robust health, less scarred by past trauma, might he have imposed sufficient discipline to inspire the most naturally gifted player of modern times to scale even loftier peaks?

At this distance – it is nearly half a century since he first pulled on a United shirt and almost four decades since he bade farewell to the Red Devils – it simply doesn't matter. For seven or eight seasons George Best gave untold pleasure to countless admirers from every corner of the globe, created so much that was ravishingly beautiful and left a hoard of precious memories. By any reasonable reckoning, that should be more than enough.

1

BAG OF BONES WITH A GOLDEN GIFT

1946 – 1961

1
BAG OF BONES WITH A GOLDEN GIFT
1946 – 1961

As the poisonous clouds of global conflict began mercifully to clear and a bright-eyed, deeply dignified new manager puffed thoughtfully on his pipe as he surveyed the bomb-ravaged Old Trafford football stadium in south-west Manchester, a boy was born to young parents Dickie and Annie across the Irish Sea, in Belfast's Royal Maternity Hospital. The first of the two new arrivals was Matt Busby, formerly an enterprising, constructive wing-half with Manchester City, then Liverpool, and now embarking on a fresh career path which was to lead to a destiny both tragic and glorious; and the baby was called George Best. Their futures were to be linked inextricably, passionately, triumphantly, if sometimes frustratingly. Together they would etch deathless chapters into the endlessly evolving history of the unique sporting institution that is Manchester United.

George entered the world on 22 May 1946, the first of Dickie and Annie Best's six offspring, whose births would be spread over the next two decades. In the immediate aftermath of war, it was a time of severe austerity, with the rationing of many staple commodities; but although the Best household was poor, it was by no means destitute, thanks to the couple's fierce work ethic and the presence of a loyal and supportive extended family. For the first two-and-a-half years of his life, the future footballing icon lived at the home of his maternal grandparents, George and Elizabeth Withers, sleeping in the converted attic in Donard Street, off Ravenhill Road in East Belfast. Not surprisingly, the youngster was immensely close to his Granda, after whom he was named, and his Granny, with whom he spent countless hours as his father and mother were so long at work.

Dickie was an iron-turner in the Harland and Wolff shipyard, alternating day and night shifts by the week; in the ceaseless battle to make ends meet Annie took a succession of part-time jobs, typically in tobacco and ice-cream factories and in a fish and chip

Even at the age of 15 months, there was the hint of an incipient body swerve.

shop. Though every hour was precious, and leisure time especially rare, the Bests were always a sporting family. Dickie played football as a pugnacious little full-back until his mid-thirties, and there had been a time when it seemed he might rise further in the game. At one point he was on the books of the eminent North Belfast side Cliftonville, the oldest club in the country and former champions of the Irish League, but in the unforgiving economic climate of the day he simply couldn't afford the lost overtime that performing regularly at that level would entail. But Dickie was not one to feel sorry for himself and he was content to turn out in the lower grade, while doing his duty by his family. For her part, Annie was a talented hockey player, only marginally short of international standard – in fact, she went for a Northern Ireland trial, only for the outbreak of war to put a temporary end to the matches, just as she would have been reaching her peak.

Thus it hardly came as any surprise when George, who had started to walk at the age of ten months, showed an early instinct for kicking a ball. Indeed, a family picture taken at around 15 months in Donard Street reveals a remarkable similarity in style to that which would later become familiar the world over. There is the crouching gait, the absolute absorption in the task at hand, the irresistible impression that the ball is utterly under the command of its diminutive master, even the hint of an incipient body swerve.

In January 1949, when George was in his third year and his new sister Carol was 15 months old, Dickie, Annie and the two children left Donard Street for a home of their own, a newly built terraced house in Burren Way, part of the sprawling Cregagh council housing estate. That was where George grew up with Carol and remained until he left for Manchester United in 1961. It was where his affinity with football mushroomed into the magnificent obsession that would lead to fame, fortune and, ultimately, dissolution and tragedy.

His love affair with the game was fanned by both his grandfathers. George Withers took him to his first game at the Hen Run, a dustbowl of a venue in Wilgar Park, and James 'Scottie' Best – the nickname a reference to his Glasgow origins – accompanied him to his first major contest. Scottie lived close to The Oval, home of Glentoran, one of Belfast's leading clubs, and while George was still tiny, in time-honoured fashion he became used to being hoisted over the turnstiles, then passed over the heads of adult supporters down to the fence, in order to get a clear view of the action. Yet for all his relish of such exciting excursions, playing football was always overwhelmingly more important to George Best than merely watching it. As he grew, at every conceivable opportunity there would be a ball at his feet, often of the tennis variety. If he had to carry a message, he would dribble all the way to his destination and all the way back, and such was the boy's devotion that when he was very young he even took his ball to bed with him.

A little later, when he became involved in kickabouts and games with other lads, all other considerations went out of the window. Sometimes his parents had to drag him indoors at bedtime, and often he would be so caked in mud from the pitch that he would have to be hosed down outside before going for a hot bath. Nothing deterred him, not even Belfast's often savage winter weather, and there were occasions when he returned home with his laces frozen solid, so that they would have to be cut away in order to remove his boots. When there were no formal games, his family always knew where to find him, either on the field behind the local sewage works or by the garages at the end of Burren Way, where he would play for hours, on his own if necessary, honing his skills ceaselessly.

A quarter of a century on, when he was playing in the United States, awed American admirers would ask him how much time he had put in to achieve his remarkable control. They were enquiring about his dedication to his craft, unfamiliar with the British culture and failing to understand that for many youngsters playing football was not just the cheapest form of entertainment, it was the only form. The fact was that any small boy from George's era and before, who was consumed by love of the game – as countless millions were – carried a tennis ball in his pocket and spent every possible moment kicking it. A wall or a door was always a welcome aid, but so adept was the scrawny Irish lad that he pinged it against uneven kerbstones, even garage doorknobs, until he could cope with every irregular deflection imaginable – which explains how, in his heyday, he was able to befuddle and infuriate opposing defenders by knocking the ball against their shins and taking the rebound. At first they thought it was luck, until he performed the same trick so many times that they realised they were the victims of sublime technique, perfected long ago on the pavements and in the alleyways of the Cregagh.

Yet, although during his days at Nettlefield primary school, near his old home with Granda and Granny Withers, George was renowned in the area as a magical manipulator of a football, there was widespread scepticism about his ability to make his living from the game because he was such a skinny bag of bones. Even his parents were convinced that he was too frail, though they knew that within those protruding ribs beat the heart of a lion. He, too, was conscious of his extreme spareness and later recounted that girls laughed at his lack of stature. That would change!

George's beloved Granda Withers had long been suffering from cancer, and died on the day George was due to sit his 11-plus examination. The family plan was to keep the demoralising news from the boy until he came home after completing his test but, on the way to school, George called at the local newsagent, where he thought the shop assistant said to him 'When is your granddad getting married?' Of course, this didn't make sense, but he thought nothing of it and went on to take his exam. Then suddenly it dawned on him that the question had actually been 'When is your granddad getting buried?' He rushed home and his darkest fears were realised. He had lost something of a soul mate, a lovely man with whom he had spent a vast chunk of his childhood, someone who had always encouraged him and spoken up for him, and he was inconsolable.

That day had another far-reaching consequence, too. An extremely intelligent boy, George was the only member of his class to pass the 11-plus, thus earning for himself a much-prized place at Grosvenor High grammar school. Though Dickie and Annie had to make sacrifices to pay for their son's new uniform and bus fares, they were exceedingly proud of his achievement and duly he started at his new school. Soon, however, he was beset by problems. He missed his old friends, all of whom were attending a secondary modern closer to home, and he was devastated that Grosvenor High played rugby to the exclusion of football. It has been written frequently that he despised the oval-ball code, but actually that was far from the truth. As a nifty and able fly-half, he did well at rugby and enjoyed it, but he just couldn't accept that there was no opportunity to play the game at which he truly excelled.

Disturbingly, too, he faced a daunting journey to and from school because his route took in a Catholic enclave and he, as his blazer proclaimed for all to see, was attending a Protestant institution. George had been brought up as a Free Presbyterian, and thus was rooted on the Protestant side of Ulster's great divide, but there was never a shred of religious bigotry about the Bests. They lived in a street where Catholics and Protestants mixed freely and happily, and at that point, in the late 1950s, the modern Troubles were not under way. Still, though, there was an undercurrent of resentment in some communities and George was subjected to a distressing daily dose of name-calling and cap-snatching that could not have been pleasant. Eventually he worked out how to time his runs to the bus stop to coincide with the vehicle pulling out, so he wouldn't have to hang around as an easy target for abuse.

As a result of all this the boy was unhappy, which was reflected in serial truancy – he had a rebellious streak even then. There was also a telling drop-off in his academic

George Best, hunched in the middle of the front row, was the undisputed star of Cregagh Youth.

performance, which was worrying because he had always shone at English and mathematics, and was potentially an outstanding student. He resorted to various ruses to skip school, including the sucking of large quantities of red wine gums to simulate tonsillitis, a devious ploy which lasted only until he was dispatched to hospital for the removal of his tonsils. In the end he was offered the choice of being demoted from the top grade at Grosvenor High or switching to Lisnaharragh Intermediate, where he could rejoin his chums and play football regularly. That proved to be one of the easier decisions George would make in his life, and soon he was thriving at the secondary modern, not only on the football pitch but in class, too.

Away from school George starred in whatever group of footballers he found himself, notably for Cregagh Youth. There wasn't an ounce of conceit in the boy, but he would have had to have been a dunce not to realise that he was way better than all his contemporaries, and regularly he distinguished himself against older and bigger opponents. He fantasised about scoring the winner in the FA Cup final for Wolverhampton Wanderers, the English team he had followed ever since seeing them in action on a neighbour's television in a series of prestigious floodlit friendlies against some of the crack continental sides, the likes of Spartak Moscow and Ferenc Puskas's Honved. That was in the days before Matt Busby and Manchester United had become pioneers in European football, and although George would never pull on the golden shirt of Wolves or figure in an FA Cup final, he and Busby would sample together the ultimate triumph any club could experience.

Still, for all his natural gifts, George continued to be widely considered too delicate and waif-like to make the grade, and it remains one of the most howling of all sporting clangers that he was never selected to play for Northern Ireland Schoolboys. Happily, however, Bud McFarlane, who ran Cregagh Youth and was also a coach with Glentoran, wasn't so sure. He had faith in the prodigy from Burren Way and arranged a match between his own team, including George, and a side of probables for the international schoolboys side. Though he was the smallest lad afield, he was the best player by far and he inspired a 2–1 victory, but still it didn't earn him that elusive cap.

Now tales of the Best prowess spread far and wide, but though legions of scouts from top clubs such as Leeds United hailed his talent, invariably they scorned his stature. With school-leaving age rapidly approaching, his father saw no alternative but to find him a job outside football, and to that end lined up a printing apprenticeship with the *Belfast Telegraph*. Even George was becoming resigned to that fate but, finally, along came a scout who recognised that some time soon the uniquely brilliant 14-year-old would fill out, and that the result would be one very special player, indeed. The seer in question was Bob Bishop, Manchester United's new man in Northern Ireland, who had already sent Jimmy Nicholson to Old Trafford and in time would add the likes of Sammy McIlroy, Jimmy Nicholl, David McCreery and Norman Whiteside to his roster of protégés.

But before he secured what would be the ultimate gem for his collection, Bishop engineered one last test. He set up a game between his own Boyland team consisting of players aged 17 and 18, men really, and a Cregagh side of which George was the creative heartbeat. His ability wasn't in question, but could he handle the physical side against boys three years his senior, most of whom seemed twice his size? It was the sort of challenge that George Best would always relish, and this time he rose to it sublimely, scoring twice and giving a fabulous all-round performance in a 4–2 victory for Cregagh. All that remained was for Bishop to phone Matt Busby and deliver perhaps the most famous one-liner in modern football history: 'I think I've found a genius.'

The Old Trafford boss had implicit faith in his shrewd Ulster representative. A donation to Cregagh of £150 was sanctioned and George was summoned from a game of street football to his house, where he found Bishop sipping a cup of tea in the front room. The next moment he was asked the question that would change his life forever: 'How would you like to play for Manchester United?'

2

ON THE THRESHOLD OF SOMETHING REMARKABLE

1961 – 1963

2
ON THE THRESHOLD OF SOMETHING REMARKABLE
1961 – 1963

By the time George Best made his first-team entrance on 14 September 1963, he had travelled a long way, literally and figuratively, from the puny and petrified schoolboy who had set out on the overnight ferry from Belfast to Liverpool in July 1961 to seek his footballing fortune with Manchester United. Although he was 15 at the time, so tiny was he – standing barely five feet without his shoes on – that until receiving the invitation from across the Irish Sea he had always worn short trousers. Thus one of the chief preparations his apprehensive mother had made for his trip was the purchase of his first pair of longs, made only after a great deal of scrimping and saving in a household where excess cash was unknown. Feeling the unfamiliar material about his knees was one strangeness, but that was nothing compared to the sheer scale of the expedition to a lad who had never previously travelled farther than 12 miles from his home city for a day at the seaside in Bangor.

He did have company – another hesitant 15-year-old Irish hopeful, Eric McMordie, a fellow trialist with Matt Busby's great club – but they were both equally unworldly and had never met before the day they waved goodbye to their parents at the Belfast dockside, so there was little sense of camaraderie to soothe their fears about what lay ahead.

As the boat ploughed through the dark waters towards England, the boys could not sleep and they arrived on Merseyside exhausted and anxious in equal measure. There

◄ This is the face that George Best showed to the world not long before he made his first-team entrance in the autumn of 1963. Not surprisingly for a 17-year-old boy a long way from home, there is still a becoming hint of naivety in those wide blue eyes, but also a dawning confidence that, at Old Trafford, he was in his element and on the threshold of something remarkable.

was no one to meet them, but somehow they made their way to Lime Street railway station and climbed aboard a train to Manchester. There was no warmer welcome at Piccadilly, which hardly reduced their rising sense of dislocation, but they were bold enough to find a taxi and asked to be conveyed to Old Trafford. Duly they were taken to the cricket ground of the same name, which baffled them at first because they had barely heard of England's summer game, let alone registered its significance in Manchester. Looking back, this appears to be unforgivably heartless and cavalier treatment by United of two kids dipping their toes into an alien environment, but maybe it was part of a deliberate hardening-up process; or possibly trialists from Ireland were so two-a-penny in the mid-twentieth century, before all the leading clubs were inundated with rookie recruits from overseas, that sometimes precious little care was taken.

On arriving at the correct Old Trafford, finally George and Eric encountered a friendly face, one belonging to United's famously avuncular chief scout Joe Armstrong, the man who had secured the services of Bobby Charlton and plenty of other household names. Inadvertently, though, he increased the pair's feelings of insecurity by well-meaningly taking them to meet several of their countrymen, including the strapping figures of goalkeepers Harry Gregg and Ronnie Briggs, and promising wing-half Jimmy Nicholson. Staring up at them, George felt there would never be a way he could force himself into a team of such muscular giants, and later he described his awe when he was presented eventually to Matt Busby: 'It was like being introduced to God,' he recalled.

Less daunting was the impression created by his prospective landlady, Mrs Mary Fullaway, a warm-hearted widow who would provide George with a comfortable haven on and off for the next nine years at her three-up three-down council house in Chorlton-cum-Hardy. Instantly she formed the opinion that George was more like a jockey than a footballer, and that he needed plenty of meat and spuds to put flesh on his bones. But before she had the chance to commence her much-needed nourishment programme, the homesick duo had run away to catch the next available ferry back to Belfast.

The decision to put a swift end to their adventure came after another near-sleepless night, during which they discussed their immediate prospects and found them unappealing. The truth was that at the time neither of them was confident about making their way in the professional game, seeing their proposed two-week trial with United as an experience that was almost certain to end in rejection. They felt lost and vulnerable, not least because most of the people they had encountered had trouble in deciphering their broad Belfast accents, and so they ran away. In George's case, it might be said that this continued a pattern which had been set by his truancy from school and was to continue later in life with serious consequences.

On the way home George felt guilty, recalling the pride and joy with which he had told his friends and neighbours of securing his big break with Manchester United. Deep down he knew that he still craved the opportunity, that he was making a mistake, and that maybe if he and Eric had been old mates, they would have egged each other on to see out the fortnight. Not surprisingly his parents were nonplussed when he turned up on the doorstep back in Burren Way, but after expressing initial astonishment, then relief that at least his son hadn't been sent home in disgrace for doing something terrible, Dickie Best played a canny game. After establishing that United would be more than ready to give him a second chance, he let George brood on what had happened, then elicited from him his own desire to return to Old Trafford. The club had talked about arranging another trial around Christmas, but for the regretful runaway that wasn't good enough. He told his father: 'No Dad, I want to go back now.' And so he did, this time on his own – and this time for keeps.

PADDY CRERAND: *The first time I saw George was at the team's hotel in London, where we were going for a banquet after winning the FA Cup in 1963. There he was, this wee fellow hanging out of the window. He looked about 12 or 13 and I thought: 'What's this boy doing at Manchester United when he should be at school?' He was actually 17 by then, and when I saw him in action on the pitch, then I knew why he was there all right. He was fantastic.*

Eventually I caught up with him in a youth match at Old Trafford. I thought to myself: 'God Almighty, what a player this little fella is!' I was sitting beside our trainer, Jack Crompton, and I said: 'Where the hell's he come from, Jack?' Jack just laughed and said: 'Oh, we're keeping him quiet! We're not telling anybody about him yet!'

He was going by people as if they weren't there. I imagine he learned that on the streets of Belfast where he was brought up. In Belfast, and Glasgow was the same, you'd be playing with about 20 kids in an enclosed area and you needed a trick or two. If you're playing in the backstreets with a crowd of working-class kids, they're going to kick you, and you learn how to avoid it. Still, he must have had an instinct for the dribbling because he was brilliant at it and not every street footballer came out like George Best.

Deep down, I think he was quite shy. Possibly there were times, much later, when he

Juggling was mainly for show, but when the training got serious, nobody at Manchester United relished it more than George Best, especially during his early years at Old Trafford before he knew for certain that he was going to make the grade.

would take a drink to bolster his confidence. He was just a little kid from Belfast, with no disrespect intended to Belfast, but he'd never been anywhere else. United's Northern Ireland scout Bob Bishop, who was a lovely man, said that.

Even in later years, no matter how draining his social exploits might have proved, Best was always ready for the hardest of graft and he was brilliant at running, faster than everyone but his pal John Fitzpatrick over long distances and Bobby Charlton over sprints.

George loved ball work the best, and often he would stay behind after everyone else had departed, endlessly practising his panoply of skills. For instance, before long it was impossible to tell which was his natural side because he had honed his left-foot deftness until it was at least the equal of his initially favoured right.

For all the reputation for unreliability that would eventually stain his copybook, essentially he was dedicated to the game, so much so that soon after arriving from Belfast he was dumbfounded to discover that some of the lads with their feet already well under the Old Trafford table and contracts in their back pockets, cheated routinely in training. When they were sent on a cross-country run, they would hide in bushes that lined an early part of the route, then rejoin the run at a later stage having doused themselves in water to simulate sweat. George didn't think it was clever, he saw it as pathetic, and he was less than astonished when most of them failed to fashion the careers their basic ability was worth.

Of course, his love affair with training had much to do with the fact that he excelled at every aspect of it, as Harry Gregg, the towering flame-haired Ulsterman – who was voted the finest goalkeeper on the planet after the 1958 World Cup finals – was to discover to his chagrin. Harry describes how his stick-thin countryman duped him and left him flailing on the grass not once, not twice, but three times during one five-a-side shortly after Best's recruitment, an episode which was to enter Old Trafford folklore.

By then George was becoming integrated into the United 'family', but initially he felt mightily frustrated by the rules of the Irish and Scottish Football Associations which prevented their youngsters signing as full-time apprentices with English clubs before they were 17. The upshot was that George, and his Aberdonian chum Fitzpatrick, had to be found outside jobs, thus restricting their training to Tuesday and Thursday nights. The little Irishman, in particular, rebelled furiously against this, moaning incessantly when he was assigned to the Manchester Ship Canal Company as a clerk. He railed so persistently against being forced to perform what he saw as menial tasks, when all he wanted was to play football, that he was switched to a timber yard, where at least he would get more exercise and be in the fresh air. However, he lasted only a morning there before walking out, and finally United were forced to find a solution that suited George and fitted the letter of the regulations, if not their spirit. They located a friendly electrical business where he was allowed to clock on in the morning, then slip out of the back door to join his mates in training, usually only returning in time to clock off at the end of the afternoon. That was a working day of which Manchester United's emerging genius thoroughly approved.

HARRY GREGG: *The first time I laid eyes on a scrawny, almost painfully shy little lad from my own country will always remain vivid in my memory. I had been taking much longer than I would have liked to bounce back from injury, so I asked the Manchester United coach Johnny Aston Senior – his son, also John, was destined to star for Manchester United when they beat Benfica to lift the European Cup in 1968 – if I could*

join in a five-a-side game with some young trialists at The Cliff training ground.

Johnny, who was a lovely man and very good at his job, might have been surprised by my request as it wasn't often that first-team players had much to do with the kids. At this point in my career I was an experienced international with Northern Ireland, having pitted my skills against many of the top marksmen in the world game and stared into the whites of their eyes as they raced towards my posts. In those circumstances, I didn't expect to be challenged mightily during this informal session with a collection of young hopefuls. Just how wrong could I be?

I hadn't been in goal for long when this dark-haired slip of a lad broke through the defence and bore down on me. Over the seasons I had developed my own way of dealing with one-on-one situations, a technique which had always worked for me in club and country confrontations around the world. As the attacker drew near and looked up in preparation for placing his shot, I would feint in one direction, then dive the other way. It was a case of seizing the initiative away from my opponent, throwing a dummy before he did it to me.

On this occasion, though, I discovered that the normal rules didn't apply. It was me who was sold a dummy as George Best ghosted past me, in that darting way of his that the world would come to know so well, and scored a goal. I was left stretched on the grass, and there was nothing for me to do but haul myself to my feet, shrug my shoulders and put it down to being ring-rusty after my lengthy lay-off. But then a few minutes later the boy wriggled free of his markers again, once more I called his bluff, thinking I was bound to catch him out this time. But the result was the same, another humiliating plunge to the turf while this cheeky little nipper waltzed past me with the ball seemingly tied to his feet.

When he had the sheer audacity to leave me in a heap for a third time I got up and told him, jokingly: 'You do that again and I'll break your bloody neck, son.' Then I had a good laugh and a chat with George and the other boys. But when I left the training ground, I couldn't forget the image of this skinny lad with the breathtaking skills. Later that day I bumped into Matt Busby at Old Trafford and, after we had chatted about my condition, I asked him if he'd seen the little lad from Belfast in action. He hadn't, so I suggested that he take a look as soon as possible. A few days later we met again and he said: 'I know the boy you mean. It's a pity he's so small.'

Soon enough the Boss was to discover that, in this case, size didn't matter. We all came to know that when he was on song, George was blessed with greatness.

Although oceans of ink and forests' worth of paper have been expended in cataloguing the extra-mural distractions that contributed to George Best's ultimate downfall, those who knew him well during his early years at Old Trafford insist, pretty well unanimously, that football was the genuine core of the young Irishman's universe. Invariably he was drawn to the game like a magnet, it was utterly irresistible to him and, at least in 1964, it defined his very being. Yet for all the phenomenal success that was ultimately to be his, it's a fact that Best was not an instant star at junior levels after overcoming his homesickness and returning to Old Trafford for a second tilt at his United windmill.

A boy and his dog – well, a friend's pooch, to be strictly accurate – pause to take in a game during a gentle Sunday morning stroll in a Manchester park, 1963.

His close pal David Sadler – born in the same year but tall and muscular, an altogether more impressive physical specimen – made far more spectacular initial progress and accordingly was rewarded with earlier promotion to the first team.

Indeed, by the spring of 1963 Best's father was getting restless at his lack of a breakthrough and was tentatively suggesting that he should go home to seek a 'proper job'. However, George was offered his contract on his seventeenth birthday in May 1963, in the run-up to a momentous occasion for the club. That week ended with United beating Leicester City in the FA Cup final at Wembley – the Irishman was a spellbound spectator in the Wembley crowd – a key milestone in Matt Busby's reconstruction work following the Munich tragedy of 1958. Soon enough, however, George would shuffle into the spotlight, diffidently at first, to pick up the torch the original Busby Babes had once wielded with such wondrous promise.

WILF McGUINNESS: *It might surprise a few people who didn't really know him, but the first thing I noticed about George Best was his shyness. I was coaching at United in the early 1960s when the word went around the staff that we had a special talent on our hands. How true that turned out to be, but my earliest impression was of a frail little chap who wouldn't say boo to a goose and who very quickly went back to Belfast because he was homesick. Mind, the impetus for that return journey across the Irish Sea came from his pal, Eric McMordie, and soon George was back at Old Trafford, making a sensational impact.*

Even then, he still resembled a matchstick boy, and he was fed a diet of steaks to build him up a bit. In those early days we nursed him as much as possible, for example sparing him most of the games in the 1963/64 FA Youth Cup campaign. By then he was already on the threshold of the first team and we didn't want him knocked about and ruined. This was often the subject of debate at the regular Sunday morning boardroom sessions called by Matt Busby to review progress at the club. The Boss was in the chair and around the table were his assistant Jimmy Murphy, trainer Jack Crompton, coach John Aston Snr, club doctor Francis McHugh, physio Ted Dalton and myself. It was wonderful for me as an impressionable twentysomething, talking informally with those great men of the game, but George was a beneficiary, too, as his development was carefully plotted.

As it turned out, the lad was more resilient, and possessed far more stamina and strength, than any of us had dreamed was possible. For all the fact that he was a mere wisp, he was as tough as whipcord and could soak up amazing amounts of physical punishment. For example, there was the time when he played four big games in the space of six days. I met him at Manchester airport on his way back from Belfast, took him to Old Trafford and let him have a brief sleep in the medical room, then sent him out to play a blinder in the decisive second leg against Swindon in the final. It was a fantastic ask of such a young boy, but George didn't bat an eyelid, just got on with it and shone as brightly as ever.

At that stage, too, he was a doddle to handle. You just told him the basics about team play and sent him out to perform. Undoubtedly there were times when he was a greedy beggar – just ask Bobby or Denis – but he had the ability to get away with it. He expressed himself, did exceptional things that were pure gold. No coach should ever stop a player from doing the unexpected. There's nothing better than that on a football pitch, and it's very rare.

3

'YOU'RE IN TODAY, SON'

1963/64

3
'YOU'RE IN TODAY, SON'
1963/64

After two years of assessment and development, Matt Busby knew that he had something special in the Belfast boy, but he wasn't going to jeopardise that limitless potential by blooding him too early at the highest club level.

When the day finally arrived for his senior entrance, the manager – not yet fully aware of George's nerveless nature – sought to protect his protégé by keeping him in ignorance of his debut until less than two hours before kick-off. The occasion was United's First Division clash with West Bromwich Albion at Old Trafford in September 1963. Ian Moir, an enormously gifted young Scot only three years Best's senior but not as resolute mentally as the Irishman would prove initially to be, had been due to wear the number seven shirt and when he fell prey to a groin injury, Busby told him to keep it a secret until the afternoon of the game. When George climbed aboard the coach taking the team to the ground, he believed he was merely a member of the squad, going along for the experience, but as the Boss strolled down the aisle he paused, leaned towards the 17-year-old and said quietly, 'You're in today, son', before ambling away.

Though it was a bolt from the blue, Best was neither fazed nor intimidated, either by the 50,000-plus crowd or his formidable direct opponent, the battle-hardened Welsh international full-back Graham Williams. Understandably the debutant took time to acclimatise, but as the game wore on he showed some delightful touches, and after the 1–0 victory he elicited this tribute from *Manchester Evening News* man David Meek, who was to become the doyen of United reporters: 'He played pluckily and finished the game in style . . . I know Matt Busby is looking forward to seeing this Belfast boy in a team with Denis Law [who was absent] to help him. I agree – it is an exciting prospect that will brighten up even the dullest of games.'

As for the lad himself, he wasn't to be carried away. Though delighted that his pal David Sadler had scored the winner, being ever the perfectionist he felt slightly deflated

What glorious days, when a top-flight footballer could enjoy a kickabout with a bunch of enthusiastic small boys in a local park. Just picture David Beckham or Wayne Rooney doing it today – it simply couldn't happen, or at least not unless access to the 'event' was strictly controlled and minutely managed. There were no such restrictions placed on George Best in the early 1960s and he threw himself into the action, risking life and limb – as a modern manager might see it – in an aerial challenge with this doughty young defender.

at his own contribution, feeling that he was capable of so much more. Thus he wasn't miffed when he returned to United's 'A' and 'B' teams to continue his soccer education. But he would be back . . .

GRAHAM WILLIAMS: *When I arrived at Old Trafford as West Bromwich Albion's left-back to face Manchester United in the autumn of 1963, I had heard plenty about the wonderboy who was due to make his debut as my immediate opponent that afternoon. His name was George Best, he was 17 years old and he was said to be brilliant, but I can't say I was worried about facing him. After all, without blowing my own trumpet, I was an experienced Welsh international and I was recognised as one of the best full-backs in the League at that time. Certainly there were no special instructions from our manager, Jimmy Hagan, who would have expected me to sort it out for myself.*

For the first ten or 15 minutes George didn't get a touch because the ball didn't come his way. Then Bobby Charlton switched to a more right-sided role, leaving George to roam, and I didn't see much more of him in that game. As I recall he just followed the ball, and it was clear that he had exceptional talent. He was thin, but he had a beautiful build, tremendous balance and a great attitude. If anybody did knock him flat – and I don't remember doing so in that game or in any of our subsequent meetings – he would bounce straight back up. He just wanted to get the ball back as quickly as possible and, certainly, he never dived in all the time I knew him. He saw it as an insult if he got kicked off the ball and he always wanted to put that right as quickly as possible. To be fair, most of the time the ball was stuck to his foot as if it was glued there. Clearly he was a fantastic athlete, seeming to glide over the ground like a thoroughbred racehorse, and as he developed he became an incredibly exciting player who would have fitted perfectly into the present Barcelona side.

At the end of one season I went on holiday to Majorca with my wife and children and George ended up babysitting for us. He was there with the actress Susan George, and although he clearly loved the socialising he never drank at all. He couldn't swim and he spent a lot of time sat on the beach, keeping an eye on the kids and chatting with my mother-in-law.

In later years when we met we always had some banter. I used to say 'It's nice to see you from the front because I was always used to watching your backside disappear along the touchline.' He would just grin and stroke his leg, saying he'd still got my autograph there.

The first of so many . . . George Best, extreme left, celebrates opening his scoring account with Manchester United in his second game, against Burnley at Old Trafford in December 1963.

As with his debut, George Best hadn't been expecting to play when he made his second appearance, against Burnley at Old Trafford three days after Christmas in 1963. He had gone home to Belfast for the holiday, but after the Reds were thrashed 6–1 by the Clarets at Turf Moor on Boxing Day, he received a telegram asking him to return to Manchester forthwith. In those days it was common for a club to face the same opponents twice in quick succession over the festive period, and now the Clarets and United were scheduled for a reverse fixture only two days later.

When the dramatic missive arrived at Burren Way, George was convinced, again, that he was needed merely to supplement the squad, but his shrewd father saw it differently. He was sure Matt Busby wouldn't have gone to so much trouble if he didn't intend

George to play, and Dickie was spot-on. Albert Quixall and Shay Brennan had been dropped, and in their place on United's flanks was the rookie pairing of George Best and the 16-year-old Merseysider Willie Anderson.

On this occasion, far from being merely untouched by the big-match atmosphere, George positively revelled in it. Indeed, before the game he displayed characteristic composure, quaffing tea at a booth in the car park with friends until half an hour before kick-off, thus causing momentary alarm to his manager, who wondered where he was – not for the last time, as it turned out!

In contrast to his previous appearance, this time Best was at the heart of the action throughout, riveting the eye as United exacted 5–1 revenge for their Boxing Day drubbing. With Bobby Charlton relishing the new deep-lying role handed to him as part of Busby's rejig, David Herd and Graham Moore provided an early two-goal lead, then George struck shortly before the interval, belting home a right-foot drive from the edge of the area, following a rare Charlton miscue. The final whistle signalled a satisfying 5–1 victory throughout which the Irishman had shone.

Precociously, perhaps, when George had received the summons, he agreed to travel only on the basis that United would fly him back to Belfast to continue his break after the match. Busby had agreed, and the next morning the local hero was out on the streets of the Cregagh, savouring the press reports of his exploits with his boyhood mates. He wasn't able to tarry long in Belfast, though, because now he was an integral part of the Manchester United first team for the foreseeable future.

Like most teenagers pitchforked into the public spotlight, George enjoyed the attention. At this point, of course, he had no concept of the publicity monster that was being created. Soon there would be a considerable wage hike, a variety of product endorsements and an unavoidable transformation in his basically normal lifestyle.

For the moment there was the local snooker hall and bowling alley, where he and his friends took advantage of a private members area because he was already starting to be noticed. A darkly handsome lad with a modest, engagingly personable air to him, George was irresistible to many of the girls who began to haunt his footsteps, and he

▶ Preparing to leave the dressing room after a match, or maybe a training session, George Best might have concluded that what he saw in the mirror was not too shabby, never mind a spot or two on his chin.

enjoyed himself to the full. Though he was no more than a light drinker at this stage, and understood why the club expected him not to be out on the town in the run-up to a game, already he preferred socialising to watching television at his digs with his roomie, David Sadler, who was the same age but a naturally relaxed, mature individual. In most situations, George Best would go his own way . . .

WILF McGUINNESS: *After spending a lifetime in the game, I can tell you of only one British team which boasted three genuinely world-class footballers at the same time. The great thing was that Bobby Charlton, Denis Law and George Best were all so very different, both in personality and in the way they played the game, and yet they complemented each other so perfectly. What they did have in common was utter self-belief. All three were modest individuals in almost every way, but when they were on the field they knew they were special, and they could nearly always find a way to express themselves through their football.*

George was a stunningly good-looking young man, and while Bobby and Denis were handsome in their own way, essentially they came from a different generation. It was the Swinging Sixties and suddenly there was a new lifestyle available to successful youngsters. Bobby and Denis were home birds, that's the way they were brought up, that's the way they lived, that's how they found happiness away from football. George was more of a townie who liked the high life. Perhaps it was unfortunate that, unlike the other two, he didn't meet somebody to fall in love with, then get married. If he had done then his whole history might have been very different.

Much is made of his drinking, and of course it destroyed him in the end, but as a teenager it wasn't noticeable. We didn't even see the girls he might have known at that stage. When the whole media circus kicked off, it was very hard for Matt Busby to deal with. He had faced worse things in his life, but this was hellish for him in a different way, and it had him scratching his head. I'm certain that he gave George plenty of fatherly advice, but it must have been hard to take that on board when so many people were opening some extremely alluring doors for him. In the end, for the lad and for Manchester United, that was the really hard part.

▶ Ten terrific young footballers and one budding genius, the Manchester United side that brought the FA Youth Cup home to Old Trafford in 1964 was richly promising. United had won the competition in the first five years of its existence with the initial wave of

Back row, left to right: Bobby Noble (captain), Peter McBride, John Fitzpatrick, Jimmy Rimmer, David Farrar, Alan Duff. Front row: Willie Anderson, George Best, David Sadler, Albert Kinsey, John Aston Jnr. Of these only McBride, Farrar and Duff failed to make a first-team appearance.

Busby Babes, showcasing such colossal emerging talents as Duncan Edwards and Bobby Charlton. But after the fifth triumph in 1957 there was a six-year hiatus as the quality of United's juniors temporarily tailed off. Now the standard had risen again, with the likes of Bobby Noble, David Sadler and John Aston Jnr. At this time Best was already playing First Division football and was not allowed to risk himself with the juniors too frequently, but he was eager to play as often as he was allowed.

DAVID SADLER: *There was nothing complicated about George, certainly not in the early years. All he wanted to do was play the game. He and I were very much of an age, signing as professionals together, eventually sharing digs for about six years and rooming together when we travelled.*

People often say we were contrasting personalities – characterising me as the quiet, sensible one – and wondered how we got on together. Well, we got on fine and George was nothing like the image people had of him. Most evenings in the earliest days we'd be playing cards or reading at home, occasionally going out for a game of snooker or ten-pin bowling. We might have the odd drink, but nothing more than a couple of halves of lager with our mates. A little later George became a regular in the team, and a huge star, while I was still on the edge of things, looking to make a permanent breakthrough. We remained close friends but gradually we moved in different social circles – I'd probably be going to the cinema with my girlfriend Christine (now my wife) while he went out clubbing.

▶ Of all the countless photographs of George Best in action during his decade of service to Manchester United, he once proclaimed this to be his favourite. The occasion is the second leg of the FA Youth Cup semi-final against Manchester City at Maine Road and United have just gone ahead 1–0 on the night, 5–1 on aggregate. What made the moment all the sweeter for the gleeful Irishman was that City's number two Mike Doyle, here throwing up his hand in disappointment, has just turned the ball into his own net, and between the two lads there was a mutual antipathy that would intensify over subsequent years. Doyle, an inspirational professional in the making but far more warrior than artist, was a vituperative United-hater and to him George personified most of what he disliked about what he perceived as the 'flashy' Reds' superiority complex. Thus this might be seen as laughing cavalier lording it over frustrated roundhead, a concept which the United man found immensely amusing.

The tie finished with George and company prevailing 8–4 over the course of the two contests, thus setting up a two-legged final with Swindon Town in which he would also excel, while being taxed to the limit by a savage schedule of four games in six days which would never be allowed in the modern era. The potentially shattering sequence demonstrated his resilience emphatically, entailing as it did a League victory over Nottingham Forest in Manchester on the Saturday; the first leg of the Youth Cup final at Swindon on the Monday, a 1–1 draw in which George scored; a second full international outing for Northern Ireland, against Uruguay on the Wednesday, which was won 3–0; and the concluding leg of the Youth Cup final, in which Swindon were eclipsed 4–1 at Old Trafford on the Thursday, with George in magical form, helping to set up a David Sadler hat-trick.

A poignant footnote – and a sadly ironic one in view of the manner of Best's ultimate demise – is that Mike Doyle, one of City's greatest ever players, died in 2011 of liver failure after years of drinking heavily.

Perusing the news in the seat behind the magnificent but frequently underrated Republic of Ireland international full-back Tony Dunne, George Best is on his way to Roker Park, Sunderland, for an FA Cup quarter-final replay in February 1964. George had scored in the original 3–3 draw at Old Trafford, then excelled in both the second match, which finished 2–2, and the 5–1 victory that settled the tie at the Leeds Road, Huddersfield. Sadly for the Red Devils, however, their progress towards Wembley was halted at the semi-final stage at a saturated Hillsborough, where they were beaten by West Ham, who went on to capture the trophy.

As a football-crazy lad growing up in Belfast, playing in an FA Cup final had been George's most ardently desired ambition, but it was one he was destined never to fulfil, even though United featured in five successive semis during the 1960s. He missed the first two, a defeat by Spurs in '62 and a victory over Southampton in '63, because he had not yet graduated to the first team. A year later, 1964, he was part of the debilitating reverse against the Hammers in the Sheffield quagmire, over which not even the light-weight Irish waif could skate, and had a role in the replayed epic against Leeds in '65, in which United were also the losers. In '66 there was yet another dismal outcome, against Everton, but this time George was missing through injury.

Even then he was only 19 years old and believed that his chance was sure to come again. So it did, in 1970, when United lost to Leeds once more, this time after three matches. But never again would arguably the finest footballer Britain has ever produced get so close to taking the stage on the gala day of the domestic game. Regrets, he had a few, and certainly in a professional sense, that was one of his biggest.

What with that disappointing FA Cup semi-final defeat by West Ham, it proved to be a campaign of near misses for Manchester United, who were runners-up to Liverpool in the title race. By now, though, Best was not only an established member of the side, but a key man and a regular match-winner. Silverware would not be long in following.

TONY DUNNE: *As Manchester United's left-back I shared the left side of the pitch with George, but in reality there wasn't any part of the pitch that he didn't think of as his own – and make his own. I couldn't blame him for that. Anybody would have done the same if they could play like that.*

George was something I'd never seen before, and have never seen since. When you're a defender you look at how the man you're marking runs with the ball. You see how and when he stops it, and how he moves it when he starts again. But with George that didn't apply. It was as though the ball was part of his foot, which meant he stopped and started again completely naturally, so that when he ran with the ball he was quicker than anybody else I've ever seen in possession. I couldn't understand how he could do it. I've never seen anything as natural as his movement, whether he was going left or right or any way he chose. It was nothing you could dream up, nothing you could have imagined . . . and to me, that was true greatness.

It was incredible for me, playing in the same team, so close to George. I loved the fact that he was on my side because I wouldn't have liked to spend the day thinking about how I might be able to stop him. When I got the ball he would usually appear next to me and I would give it to him. How could I go wrong? Matt Busby told me to give it to him more and more, and it paid off.

People used to kick him. There were a lot of top-quality full-backs in the British game, none of them afraid to get stuck in, but his attitude to taking physical punishment was fantastic. At times I'd worry about him because he was so slim, but you didn't have to worry. I'd look at his leg, see a horrible bruise with blood oozing out of it, and I'd ask him how he was. 'Aw, it's nothing TD, I'll be fine,' he'd say. George understood that full-backs had to have a go at him, that it was their job, and he accepted it without moaning.

George made me realise what it takes to be a great footballer. He made me understand that if anyone was to be judged in that category then they had to be as good as him. Now, I would have considered myself as very, very lucky to have played with one like that during my career, but I was blessed – I played with three. I couldn't separate Bobby Charlton, Denis Law and George Best. They were all out of this world, and I saw my job as winning the ball and giving it to them.

The three of them were such lovely fellas, too, in their different ways. George was charming. At first I thought he couldn't have known how good he was, he was that nice, that modest. But he did, and he was still charming. A lot of people said George was the best thing since sliced bread. Well, I reckon he was better than sliced bread!

◄ A wholehearted but scrupulously fair challenge between two noted bon viveurs, although at this point in the spring of 1964, George was only a green beginner in the socialising stakes. Not so the fellow in the act of dispossessing him of the ball, Fulham's flamboyant centre-half Bobby Keetch, an unmissable figure with his immaculately coiffured blond thatch and swashbucklingly aggressive style.

It was often said of Keetch, an engaging character who was popular throughout the game, that the more gilded the reputation of an opponent, the bigger the boots he would wear for the occasion. As for George, he relished a battle, too, taking on hulking markers with the same eagerness and sense of adventure that he had taken into his street games back in Belfast. On a March afternoon at Craven Cottage, honours finished even with the score at two apiece.

4
WONDER BOY
1964/65

4
WONDER BOY
1964/65

The world was changing for Manchester United at the dawn of the 1964/65 campaign, with major reconstruction progressing on two fronts. Old Trafford was about to acquire a striking modern look in time to accommodate the likes of Brazil, Hungary and Portugal for the 1966 World Cup finals, which would mean much of that familiar imposing industrial backdrop on the edge of Trafford Park being obscured behind a new cantilevered north stand running down the far side of the ground from the tunnel. Thus Kirtley's lard factory, complete with its eye-catching steeple capped by a jaunty weather vane, would no longer add a certain dramatic dimension to routine photographs of football action, and the arena would acquire a much more enclosed atmosphere.

More importantly, Matt Busby had almost completed his post-Munich rebuilding job on the pitch, his team evolving at last into a truly impressive edifice to match the stadium. After what had always felt like a false dawn in 1958/59, when United had valiantly bucked the odds by finishing as First Division runners-up only 15 months on from the tragedy, there had been a sobering reality check, with a descent first into mid-table and then further into the lower reaches, so that in 1963 even relegation had seemed possible. But now, more than half a decade on from that calamitous afternoon on a snowy Bavarian runway, Busby had achieved a satisfying balance. The shrewd, velvet-voiced Scot, while still suffering his own severe physical repercussions from the accident, had assembled a tightly knit rearguard, an upliftingly creative midfield and an exciting attack which could shred any opposition. Finally the Red Devils were ready to take on the very best once again, and they proved it by winning the League title for the first time since the disaster.

Of the team only two men, Bill Foulkes and Bobby Charlton, had tasted first-team action before Munich while only a couple more, Shay Brennan and Nobby Stiles, had

Lining up from left to right, back row: Jack Crompton (trainer), Bill Foulkes, David Sadler, Pat Dunne, Shay Brennan, Graham Moore, Paddy Crerand, Noel Cantwell, Matt Busby (manager). Front row: John Connelly, Nobby Stiles, Bobby Charlton, Denis Law, Tony Dunne, David Herd, George Best.

even been on the club's books at the time. Many of the rest had been expensive transfer acquisitions, but none of them would make a more seismic impact than the slim little fellow with the dark hair and the demure expression on the right of the front row. He had risen, practically unheralded, through the youth ranks. Now was his time.

DAVID HERD: *Playing up front in a side containing George Best, Denis Law and Bobby Charlton was a privilege, better than anything I could have dreamed of. When any of them got the ball the other team never knew what to expect. In George's case, we had no idea what was coming either, so what chance did our opponents have?*

GEORGE COHEN: *Because I was the full-back and George Best was the winger, most people might assume that I was breaking up a Manchester United attack here, but actually I was attacking down the right touchline myself and he was making a tackle on me. In fact, that often happened because I loved to overlap, and George was one of those wingers who was not afraid to track back and make a challenge.*

Of course, when he did go forward I have to admit that he was a pretty fair performer! To give him his due, he was one of the greatest wingers I ever faced, always trying to get me off balance, to send me the wrong way, and then dart past with the ball. I had to be thinking the whole time. I did my best to open up a wing for him, to lead him where I knew he would run out of space, all the while getting my body in the right position to make my tackle.

A thousand things go through your mind during a game, and with experience you try to read the play better, to save energy. But a player like George Best could always come up with the unexpected to keep you on your toes.

Like the Welsh flier Cliff Jones, another wonderful winger who starred for Spurs when they won the League and FA Cup double in 1961 and later played with me at Fulham, George was extremely brave, never pulling out of any physical challenge. That was the only way he knew how to play, doubtless having been brought up in a hard school on the streets of Belfast, as was Cliff in Swansea. If either of them had the slightest sight of goal, they would go for it with everything they had. They could never have been shrinking violets and been the wonderful footballers that they were. They stood up for themselves against defenders, they took the knocks and they didn't get the protection that players get today. Invariably if George had been flattened he would just get up and get on with the game, and there would be a sincere handshake at the end. Not that I ever tried to be heavy-handed with him, you understand. I wasn't going to be nasty!

What made George particularly tricky to face was the timing of his runs and his fantastic balance. Like Bobby Charlton, his teammate with United and mine with England, he had electrifying speed over the first 15 yards, which made him difficult to pin down. All great footballers – and he was certainly in that category – have that little something extra. Nobody could ever play him out of the game completely. You might think you had, then suddenly he would do something special and leave you standing.

Off the pitch I remember George as a very nice young man, and it was extremely generous of him to say I was the best full-back he had faced. I hope he hadn't drunk too much at the time!

George Best, already a regular in the Manchester United side at the age of 18, does battle with Fulham right-back George Cohen in the early autumn sunshine in front of a shirtsleeved crowd at Craven Cottage in September 1964.

In 1964, Cohen, one of the hardest and most efficient defenders of his generation, had just earned his place in the England team. His performance against Manchester United at Craven Cottage in that September was one that would convince national boss Alf Ramsey that the pacy Londoner was a man who could help to deliver the World Cup on home soil in 21 months' time. Neither for the first nor the last time, Ramsey's judgement proved impeccable.

Best found Cohen such a formidable opponent because the Fulham right-back played him with a rare mixture of intelligence and brawn, and because whenever possible he forced the United man on the defensive by making attacking runs of his own.

The Cottagers, who would only narrowly avoid relegation after finishing 27 points adrift of Matt Busby's champions, nevertheless won this game 2–1, after which they were above United in the table. The visitors dominated territorially, but they were creatively sluggish and although Best himself was sparky, his fellow stars Bobby Charlton and Denis Law were struggling to find their early-season form. Defeat was particularly frustrating as the Red Devils had taken the lead through winger John Connelly shortly before the interval, but then conceded a freak own-goal by Shay Brennan and allowed Fulham's sublimely gifted midfield general Johnny Haynes to seal a surprise victory with

Nottingham Forest's Joe Wilson goes to ground in his attempt to deal with George Best at Old Trafford in September 1964, but although the pugnacious little full-back stuck to his task with admirable tenacity, he endured a torrid afternoon against United's emerging genius.

a soft shot near the end.

In the same month, against Nottingham Forest at Old Trafford, the hosts won 3–0, through two goals from centre-forward David Herd and one from flankman John Connelly, to set off on a sequence of 13 wins and a draw that would lift them to the top of the table. Though he didn't make the scoresheet, Best was United's outstanding performer, always seemingly on the verge of breaking through the Forest back line. Most of the chances he created that day were missed by his colleagues, but he had served notice of his talent and soon he was to become a marked man. Unlike many wingers, George was rarely content to hug his touchline, thereby drifting on the periphery of the action for lengthy periods. Instead, usually, he adopted a roaming brief, and if the ball didn't come to him then he would scamper energetically to all corners of the pitch until he located it. Matt Busby, wise man that he was, didn't discourage his prodigy in this. The United manager had always believed in giving gifted youth its head, as exemplified by his Babes in the previous decade, and now he found himself in charge of such a unique talent, there was no way he was going to shackle it.

Accordingly he asked his right-hand man, the inspirational, often abrasive yet fundamentally golden-hearted Jimmy Murphy, to put out the word to the entire coaching and training staff that nobody should attempt to change the natural Best style. The former Welsh international needed no second bidding. As a fire-and-brimstone wing-half with West Bromwich Albion before the Second World War, he had taken no prisoners, and now he recognised, and relished, that same hunger in George Best. As he put it: 'If a movement breaks down he is one of the few forwards who has this surge of annoyance and he comes racing back, snapping for the ball like a terrier. He hates losing the ball, and to see that in a player with such fantastic natural ability is truly rare – and I love it!'

Best's form during the autumn of 1964 was frequently scintillating, never more so than at the Stamford Bridge home of championship rivals Chelsea. United won 2–0, a significant staging post in the battle for the crown, but it was the dazzling display of Best rather than the team's gathering momentum that created the next day's headlines. Tommy Docherty's thrusting young side, in which Terry Venables supplied many of the attacking ideas and the muscular likes of Ron Harris and Eddie McCreadie were bastions of the defence, and which had itself compiled a ten-match unbeaten sequence since the outset of the season, were run ragged by the slender Irishman. Ken Jones, a widely respected *Daily Mirror* man, compared Best to such legends of the game as Stanley Matthews and

Still looking slim, almost frail, in United's change kit of all-white with red facings at Burnley in October, George Best warms up ahead of kick-off. The game, in which the Red Devils' former Clarets favourite John Connelly was made skipper for the day, finished goalless, representing the sole dropped point in a 14-match sequence stretching from mid-September to the end of November.

the Brazilian Garrincha, and there was a telling absence of demurring voices.

After surviving a spirited early buffeting from the Pensioners – as they were nicknamed at the time, these days preferring the Blues as a tag less open to abuse – United took control before half-time through a stunning piece of opportunism by Best, who seized on a rare slip by McCreadie to clip the ball past goalkeeper Peter Bonetti. Then, about a quarter of an hour from the final whistle, the Reds' quicksilver number 11 set up the clincher for Denis Law, sealing a crucial 2–0 victory. When the game was over, players from both teams joined the majority of the captivated crowd in standing to clap the young man from the arena and he walked off, head bowed and seemingly embarrassed, but actually stirred to the depths of his soul by what he had done. Paddy Crerand, always a man for a colourful turn of phrase, later spoke of Best leaving his direct opponent, the classy Ken Shellito, with 'twisted blood' through his repertoire of coruscating footwork.

It was a memorable description of an unforgettable performance, which had a profound effect on George himself. Later he would say that it was after his evisceration of poor Shellito at the Bridge that it fully dawned on him that he might ascend to the game's giddiest heights, that true stardom was beckoning.

When the two teams met again in March, absence through injury spared the England international Shellito from another runaround, but Best was in the same merciless mood as Chelsea were hammered 4–0. This time it took him only three minutes to open the scoring, in front of the Stretford End, and it was a goal fit for the gods. McCreadie attempted a clearance, which Best charged down near the byline on the left, then the harassed defender lost control of the ball as he tried to turn it back towards his keeper, Bonetti. George nipped in, and might have opted for a cross to the well-positioned Denis Law or David Herd in the centre, but instead of the merely brilliant he executed the sublime, curling the ball into the far side of the net with his right foot from a remarkably acute angle.

If that was the high point of an incandescent display, it was not the end of the Best magic as he set up goals for Law and Herd. Although Chelsea were still three points clear of Busby's men, and Don Revie's

Wearing the blue kit United sometimes favoured when they travelled to face opponents in red, the teenage George Best looks as if butter wouldn't melt in his mouth ahead of the 3–2 victory over Arsenal at Highbury in November 1964.

A more recognisable image to his would-be shadowers in the Gunners defence, however, is this, where he is swaying beguilingly in the face of yet another challenge with the ball seemingly glued to his right boot.

rugged and tenacious Leeds were not to be discounted, the title tide had turned decisively.

Best was on formidable form against Arsenal at Highbury in November 1964, his sleight of foot bamboozling the thoroughbred England international full-back Don Howe. He was a cultured performer approaching the veteran stage, and as a man who would go on to become one of the outstanding coaches of his generation he must have appreciated the sheer virtuosity of his tormentor, while ruing the sorry circumstance of being detailed to subdue him.

With Best tripping the light fantastic in front of nearly 60,000 spectators, and Denis Law at his most deadly, United were three up inside half an hour, with the impish Scot striking twice and Connelly once. But to be fair to Billy Wright's dogged side, they refused to grovel and struck back through Terry Anderson and an inspired George Eastham to force a tense finish. United ended the afternoon three points clear at the First Division's summit and the impetus towards a first championship since Munich continued to gather pace.

There was nothing of the natural show-off about George Best, however. Oh, he realised, probably during the 1964/65 season, that he was a truly exceptional footballer, but he remained an essentially modest lad and he wasn't one to rub an honest opponent's nose in the mud. Yet there was always about him a sense of the theatrical, an element of the showman, and that surfaced vividly during Manchester United's FA Cup fifth-round clash with Burnley at Old Trafford in February 1965.

Making a mockery of the formbook, Matt Busby's side was a goal down to the mid-table Clarets as the clock ticked past the 80-minute mark, that battle-scarred gladiator Andy Lochhead having supplied the only goal of the contest in the first half. But then George, who had lost his left boot in a fearsome challenge with a Burnley de-

fender, elected to take a pass when the ball appeared at his feet, playing on with only half the regulation footwear. He might have been hopelessly incapacitated, but he wasn't, instead taking a touch and delivering a beautiful cross from which Denis Law equalised with a trademark bicycle kick.

Even then, there was another idiosyncratic contribution to come from the Irishman. Playing on with one boot, the action being too frenetic to enable him to be re-shod, next minute he sneaked away from marker Fred Smith and delivered the cross from which Paddy Crerand struck a dramatic winner.

Come the final whistle, still clutching his boot in one hand, he held out his other to shake with poor Smith (above). George was grinning broadly, but there was no undue triumphalism, just a wry recognition that something extraordinary had taken place. He was different from the norm, a fact that the world was just beginning to realise.

At this point United seemed to be a fair bet for the League and FA Cup double, a feat

then achieved only once before in the twentieth century, by Bill Nicholson's gloriously free-flowing Tottenham Hotspur in 1960/61. But although the Red Devils cuffed aside Wolves 5–3 in the quarter-finals after being two goals down in the first 15 minutes, they went out to title rivals Leeds in the last four after two bone-crunchingly attritional contests.

Though Leeds and Chelsea were Manchester United's main challengers for the First Division crown in 1964/65, the gut-deep rivalry that would grow to colossal and often poisonous proportions was with Liverpool, the reigning champions managed by Matt Busby's countryman and close pal Bill Shankly.

When the two sides had met at Anfield on Hallowe'en, the Merseysiders were a shadow of their title-winning selves of the previous season, already way off the pace in the new term's race and, after United had triumphed 2–0, no less canny a judge than the great Tom Finney – trumpeted by Shankly as the finest player he had ever seen – had lauded the contributions of Denis Law, Bobby Charlton and, most heartfelt of all, 'the wonder boy George Best'. 'The Preston Plumber' described the diminutive Irishman as a natural who commanded the eye, and who had the invaluable knack of remaining calm in a crisis.

Come the rematch on Easter Saturday, United were locked in a tense race with Leeds for the top prize in the domestic game, with Liverpool well adrift – they would finish in a distant seventh place. In such circumstances, nerves might get the better of the team with the most to lose, but when Shankly brought his troops to Old Trafford, United triumphed with a comfort that bordered almost on disdain.

Key to the hosts' emphatic 3–0 win was yet another livewire performance from George Best, who had netted twice five days earlier in an important 4–2 win at Birmingham. He popped up in all attacking areas, darting dangerously into space and causing constant problems for a hard-pressed Liverpool rearguard, as in this wriggling assault in front of the Stretford End (top left). Though he riveted the attention of his opponents (from left to right, Willie Stevenson, goalkeeper Tommy Lawrence, Gerry Byrne and Geoff Strong), most of the time they struggled even to get close to him. However, he proved unable to force an early breakthrough – it looks as though both he and Denis Law were offside in this sortie (bottom left) – and it needed a piece of characteristic opportunism from the quicksilver Scot to shatter the visitors' disciplined resistance shortly before the break.

Thereafter United's football flowed more freely, with Best in particular expressing himself entertainingly, but it took a brace of clever set-ups by the inventive Paddy Crerand

Clearly this was not a moment of unalloyed joy for Bobby Charlton, Denis Law and George Best as they trudge from the Old Trafford arena after a particularly unfulfilling session in the mid-1960s.

to fashion further successful strikes by John Connelly and Law. The victory was rapturously received by the Old Trafford multitude, who could now sense that their eight-year wait for the championship was almost at an end.

It was a fact not always understood by the fans at the time that the glorious trinity of Charlton, Law and Best, although they worked together closely as comrades in the common cause, were vastly differing personalities who could hardly be expected to be the best of buddies away from the game.

For a start Bobby and Denis, respectively nine years and six years the Belfast boy's senior, were effectively from a different generation to George, and they were married men with families while he remained young, unattached, emphatically fancy-free. That led to a fundamental contrast in their way of life, a gap that would never be bridged during their playing days.

That said, George was always closer to Denis than he was to Bobby, whom he went through a period of resenting, seemingly because of the older man's rigid sense of duty towards the club. Their subsequent reconciliation, though, by the time of George's death meant that they were better friends than at any previous period of their lives.

At the end of only his first full season as a Manchester United regular, still three days short of his nineteenth birthday, George Best paraded the League championship trophy around Old Trafford, aided and abetted by Nobby Stiles (overleaf), the ferociously combative wing-half destined to become a World Cup winner with England some 14 months later.

Matt Busby's third outstanding United side – the first was the 1948 FA Cup winners and multiple title runners-up, the second consisted of the Busby Babes – had realistically assured themselves of the prize by beating Arsenal 3–1 under the Old Trafford lights in the campaign's penultimate game. After that it would have taken a 19–0 defeat at Aston Villa in their final outing to prevent them becoming champions, and not even the most pessimistic of their fans could have considered that outcome possible.

Before meeting the Gunners, though, there was a worry over the fitness of leading scorer Denis Law, who was limping along with six stitches in a knee wound suffered in the recent victory over Liverpool. Contrary to popular belief that the plucky Scot was consumed with eagerness to play, actually he was more than ready to sit out the action while nursing the throbbing joint, but his manager insisted he'd be all right on the night so he had little choice in the matter.

As it turned out, that supreme psychologist Matt Busby could hardly have made a more prescient call. As soon he was on the pitch Denis, as much a warrior as any man who ever wore the red shirt, banished the pain from his mind and proceeded to set up the first goal for George after only six minutes. As Frank McGhee recorded in the *Daily Mirror*: 'Law, twisting on that injured knee to avoid a tackle, slipped the ball to Best. The kid trapped it calmly, swivelled towards goal, paused almost cheekily as if to examine the situation, and then shot past Arsenal keeper Jim Furnell.'

As the evening wore on, the decision to press Law into action proved increasingly inspired. Just short of the hour mark he doubled United's lead from close range, then after George Eastham induced mild tremors by pulling one back – they were only mild because

there had been an announcement that the Reds' only title rivals, Leeds, were three down at Birmingham – Denis grabbed the clincher from a Best corner. Even though Leeds fought back to draw at St Andrew's, United were the new champs barring a collapse of impossible proportions at Villa Park, and the Old Trafford dressing room was awash with champagne. But not for George, the boss decreeing that such a young lad should stick to lemonade.

A public celebration with the silverware was delayed, however, until the Reds entertained the French club, Strasbourg, more than three weeks later in the second leg of the Inter-Cities Fairs Cup quarter-final. Though there were no goals that night, Busby's boys won 5–0 on aggregate, only to lose a bad-tempered semi to the crack Hungarian side Ferencvaros after three matches. Thus the season didn't end until the 16th of June, after which George went off to enjoy what remained of the summer while, gently at first, the publicity machine dedicated to lionising football's rising star began to crank itself up.

NOBBY STILES: *George is looking a wee bit chirpier than me here. Perhaps I'm struggling to keep up with him, because he was like lightning.*

5

'EL BEATLE' SHREDS THE SCRIPT

1965/66

Pencil-slim and somehow vulnerable, with a becoming dark curl tumbling across that handsome brow, George Best is snapped in profile during a break of play in the home game with Blackburn Rovers in November 1965.

5
'EL BEATLE' SHREDS THE SCRIPT
1965/66

I n 1965, George was emerging as the perfect poster boy as a new generation of football fans who embraced that decade's explosion of youth culture sought a sporting equivalent of the Beatles. At first it was fabulous fun, and he revelled in the attention, but there was no precedent within the world of football to indicate how a lad might deal with the situation. Certainly George didn't have the slightest idea how to cope, and it was no good turning for advice to senior players, the likes of Bobby Charlton and Denis Law, because such intense personal adulation was an alien concept to them. Matt Busby and everyone else at Old Trafford were at a loss, too, and eventually both Manchester United and the Irishman would pay a grievous price for what was, to be fair to all concerned, an understandable lack of relevant experience. Much of the constant media attention was essentially good-humoured, but some of it was crassly intrusive. He would have to become accustomed to *that* for the rest of his days.

Raindrops keep falling on my head . . . George Best looks bedraggled and a tad forlorn on the pitch at Turf Moor, Burnley, in September 1965, and it was understandable if he wasn't too happy with the afternoon's work. The Clarets beat the reigning champions 3–0, leaving them with only two victories in their first seven League games, way off the pace in their bid to retain the title.

▲ On the pitch, though, Best could be virtually untouchable. Here, surrounded by a seemingly impenetrable thicket of defenders, somehow he retains both the ball and the initiative. This image, which was taken during Manchester United's 5–2 FA Cup victory over Derby County at the Baseball Ground on a murky Saturday afternoon in January 1966, is an apt illustration of the Irishman's near-uncanny knack of keeping possession in virtually any circumstances. His skill was quite astonishing, his downright physical toughness was often underrated and his balance was sublime, a combination of attributes which so frequently proved irresistible. On this occasion, both George and Denis Law scored twice, with David Herd contributing United's fifth.

◄ Here is George Best at his most unstoppable, running half the length of Molineux to score against Wolves in the FA Cup in March 1966. He appears to float above the mud and although the ball is bouncing it remains under perfect control. Opponents and teammates alike struggled to keep pace with the Irishman in this mood. Would-be marker Joe Wilson (left) is trailing in his wake while David Herd, United's number 10, waits in vain for a pass that will never come. The boot on the right belongs to the experienced defender Ron Flowers, but George merely veered to his right to elude the England man before stroking a low shot beyond the reach of Wolves keeper Dave MacLaren, whose desperate plunge to his left was in vain.

Any annoyance at not receiving the ball forgotten in the sheer euphoria of the moment, David Herd prepares to embrace the cavorting scorer (below). This was the type of goal that George Best relished the most, one which involved him appearing to take on the other team single-handed, then overcoming the odds to plonk the ball in the net. It was a golden individualistic effort which summed up his unique appeal.

It was a strike, too, which brought smiles of appreciation even to the faces of some of the Wolves fans behind the goal. For them it was a moment of raw disappointment after their side had led through two early penalties by Terry Wharton, only to be pegged back by a couple of Denis Law headers before the Best masterpiece had put the Reds in front some 20 minutes from the end. But still, deep down, they understood that they had been privileged witnesses of something special. As for the faithful and often underrated Herd, his patience was rewarded by a goal shortly before the final whistle, sealing the visitors' 4–2 victory and their place in the FA Cup quarter-finals.

Put it there, pal. Eusebio of Portugal and Northern Ireland's George Best exchange greetings at Old Trafford before kick-off in the first leg of the European Cup quarter-final between Manchester United and Benfica in February 1966.

Two of the finest footballers of all time and the most eminent from each of their respective countries, Eusebio and Best met at Old Trafford in February 1966 in the European Cup quarter-final. At that point the mighty Eagles of Lisbon were one of the premier powers in world football, having appeared in four out of the previous five European Cup finals and won two of them, with Eusebio, the 'Black Panther', indisputably their main man. He was at his zenith – Denis Law would present him with the European Footballer of the Year trophy ahead of the quarter-final second leg, and he would go on to star for Portugal in that summer's World Cup finals in England. Now, for the first time but not the last, he was identified as the chief threat to United's European ambitions.

That night in Manchester the hosts – looking like Real Madrid in their all-white strip in an era when it was not always the away team which changed colours in the event of a clash – claimed an important victory, though arguably it was the visitors who were most satisfied with the 3–2 scoreline. Jose Augusto put Benfica in front early on, but then an exquisitely perceptive Best delivery set up David Herd for an equaliser before goals from Law and Bill Foulkes put United in charge with half an hour to play. However, the irrepressible Eusebio created the opening for Jose Torres to prod the ball into Harry Gregg's net, and at the end the general verdict was that Matt Busby's side needed rather more than a fragile one-goal advantage if they were going to prevail in Lisbon five weeks later. Indeed, as they strode off the pitch at the final whistle, Eusebio and company were already grinning like victors.

For all those with Manchester United in their hearts, or indeed for any sane observer equipped with a basic appreciation of sporting excellence regardless of partisan allegiance, the night of the second leg was one to treasure. The Estadio da Luz played host to a spontaneous eruption of incandescent shimmering beauty as the 19-year-old George Best danced and dazzled under the Lisbon lights like some crazed unquenchable firefly, in the process redefining what was possible against one of the great European powers in their own formidable stronghold. As Benfica were eclipsed to the barely believable tune of 5–1, the handsome Manchester matador gave the performance of his life to date, and although he turned on countless inspirational displays for United over the next half a dozen or so campaigns, it was one he never equalled.

Remarkably, this awesome individual exhibition, which inspired his teammates into arguably United's finest collective effort since the Munich disaster, came only a few months after the Irishman had been axed for three games because Matt Busby, even at that early stage of the Irish wisp's career, thought he was indulging in too many late nights. When he had omitted Best for the first leg of their European Cup preliminary round encounter with HJK Helsinki in Finland, he had reflected, rather optimistically as events were to prove: 'I'm sure the lapse was only temporary.' As for George, he had owned up cheerfully to his mild misdemeanour, admitting that he had, indeed, been finding it difficult to concentrate on his game, an ominous foretaste of what was to come in later years.

Before the second meeting with Benfica, given United's fearfully slim advantage against such a dynamic attacking force as Eusebio, Torres and company, Busby had counselled early caution. Though United were renowned for their swashbuckling approach, on this occasion he advised a policy of containment and consolidation for the first 20 minutes until his men had bedded into the game. Someone, it would transpire, might not have been listening!

With the notable exception of the almost preternaturally cool George Best, the Red Devils were uncharacteristically tense before kick-off, knowing how dearly their manager cherished the ambition of lifting the trophy which meant so much to him after so many of his Babes had lost their lives in its pursuit eight years earlier. Shortly before leaving the dressing room Paddy Crerand had accidentally shattered a mirror by miskicking

a football, an incident which played on already taut nerves. As they crossed the white line they were greeted by a barrage of noise from some 75,000 fans, the feverish effect heightened tumultuously by fireworks which fizzed and soared around the imposing stadium.

There was barely a pause in the pandemonium as Denis Law, the previous European Footballer of the Year, handed his successor, Eusebio, the award in a ceremony which some observers from the visiting camp reckoned was calculated to emphasise Benfica's stature and ram home their supposed advantage before the 90 minutes ahead. The scale of United's task was illustrated by the fact that the Eagles had never been beaten in European competition on their own turf, winning 18 games and drawing one while tallying 78 goals with only 13 in reply. Never had foreign visitors scored more than two

on the ground and to say that the Portuguese were confident of overturning a 3–2 deficit was a massive understatement.

Benfica began brightly enough, but after six minutes their script was shredded. Bobby Charlton was body-checked near the left touchline, Tony Dunne floated over a free-kick which seemed to hang tantalisingly in the air, then George Best leapt above a gaggle of lanky defenders to dispatch a perfect looping header beyond the despairing clutch of goalkeeper Costa Pereira. George had always been brilliant in the air for such a skinny little fellow, but this time he excelled himself, partly due to his phenomenal natural athleticism but with a grateful nod, also, to interminable practice sessions under one of the Old Trafford stands in which a ball was hung from a girder on a piece of string, and was lifted higher each time the Irishman managed to reach it with his head.

As Best turned to celebrate ecstatically with the jubilant Denis Law (left), Pereira could only look on ruefully while full-back Domiciano Cavem was prone and dejected on the edge of the six-yard box. Thus did the Eagles' wings receive an unexpected early clipping, but even then they could never have imagined the comprehensive plucking of their magnificent plumage that lay ahead.

Only another six minutes had elapsed – that's a dozen altogether – when a long punt from United's net-minder Harry Gregg was nodded by David Herd into the path of the dashing Best, who set off on a mazy slalom that took him gliding beyond three Benfica challenges, which were bypassed with the effortless elan of a champion skier rounding a collection of fenceposts. Costa Pereira stuttered from his line to confront the audacious sprite, but he was unable to repel a flashing low cross-shot from just inside the box (below). Suddenly the hosts were 2–0 down on the evening, 5–2 on aggregate, but their nightmare was only just beginning.

Their gloom deepened only four minutes later when Law and Best combined sweetly to send in John Connelly for a third goal and Benfica's hopes were pretty well extinguished.

The rampant Irishman even found the net a third time but was judged marginally offside, a shame because no display was ever more deserving of a hat-trick. Still, he continued to shine at the heart of a glorious team performance that combined fluent mobility, sublime skill and controlled aggression. An own-goal by full-back Shay Brennan, who lobbed a backpass over the head of the advancing Gregg, reduced the arrears on 52 minutes, but the masterful Crerand plundered United's fourth after 80 minutes, then Charlton waltzed gracefully through the Portuguese's shell-shocked rearguard to stroke a fifth a minute from the end. That completed what was in 1966, and arguably remains today, the most impressive display by a British team on foreign soil, just as George Best's contribution surely still stands as the most sensational individual effort from any footballer from these islands in the continent's premier competition.

All four goal-scorers performed admirably, but there was no doubt which one was going to hog the headlines for the foreseeable future, especially when Matt Busby revealed that his pre-match team talk had urged a careful approach. As he put it, grinning broadly: 'George must have had cotton wool in his ears when we made our plans. I wish he wouldn't listen to me a bit more often!'

In fact, it wasn't that Best had wilfully disobeyed his manager, merely that opportunities had presented themselves and he had seized them, in the process leaving tactical convention in ruins.

It was the day on which George Best's life changed forever, the morning after he had put the mighty Benfica to the sword more comprehensively than could ever have been dreamed

Having showered and dressed, the four scorers in Manchester United's defeat of Benfica line up for an enterprising cameraman who has slipped into the Stadium of Light dressing room. Indulging in a little richly deserved light refreshment are, left to right, John Connelly, Paddy Crerand, George Best and Bobby Charlton.

possible. Unwittingly or not, as he strolled the streets of Lisbon with his old youth team chum John Fitzpatrick and David Herd (opposite), he was entering an entirely new realm of public exposure. Having already been dubbed 'El Beatle' in match reports, he played up to the starry image by buying the biggest sombrero he could find, then sporting it not only on his triumphant perambulation around the Portuguese capital, but also on his return to Manchester airport later that day. It was the perfect picture opportunity for the snappers who awaited his arrival and duly it was splashed on the front pages of newspapers all over Europe.

It would be hard to deny that he relished the adulation, but in his defence it should be pointed out that the teenager from Burren Way had no way of understanding the media monster he was creating. From here on, everybody would want a piece of George Best, quite literally in the case of the fan who approached him brandishing a fearsome knife as he walked off the pitch at the end of the Benfica match. Luckily on that occasion, the fellow was only after a souvenir lock of his hair. In the years to come, there would be no shortage of voracious pressmen who wanted blood.

It was in the FA Cup quarter-final draw against Preston North End in March 1966 that Best suffered an injury that would both seriously damage Manchester United's prospects for the rest of the season and have undesirable long-term consequences for his own career. Having danced his way past a number of opponents, he was brought down in a clumsy, but not malicious, tackle from behind, suffering a serious knee cartilage injury in the process. Because he was such a vital player to the Red Devils' aspirations in all three major competitions, Matt Busby decided that the injury should be managed, with the necessary operation being postponed, perhaps even until season's end. Accordingly George was sidelined for the replay, in which Preston were beaten 3–1 at Old Trafford, and the next League game, a 1–1

draw at Aston Villa.

Then, with European and FA Cup semi-finals in prospect, he was tried in the First Division visit of Leicester, which ended in a depressing 2–1 defeat, and although he was clearly incapacitated by the pain, he was picked for the last-four clash with Partizan Belgrade. That afternoon in Yugoslavia he took a fearful physical battering from opponents who had been well and truly alerted to his quality by his starring display in Lisbon, but such were his appetite for the game and his hunger to please Busby, he contrived to be the most dangerous United man on the field. Unfortunately, his courage was not enough as United, with several other players also performing with injuries that should have seen them on the treatment table rather than the pitch, nosedived to a dismal 2–0 reverse.

That proved to be George's last game of 1965/66 as he underwent the much-needed knee operation; although he would return to fabulous form, he would always suffer twinges that arguably fuelled the frustration which would engulf him for different reasons in the years ahead. The immediate upshot for United was a calamitous loss of sparkle and invention that saw them fall away limply in the League – in all honesty, they had never looked like matching Liverpool that term – and turn in jaded displays in the big cup competitions. With the even younger Willie Anderson in George's place, the Reds beat Partizan 1–0 at Old Trafford, thus going down 2–1 on aggregate, and then fell flat in the FA Cup semi-final, losing 1–0 to Everton at Burnden Park.

It's impossible to be certain, but with a fit George Best Manchester United would have been strong favourites to lift both knockout trophies. As it was even the dignified Busby despaired, declaring: 'We'll never win the European Cup now!' Meanwhile George had to be content with third place in the European Footballer of the Year poll, behind clubmate Bobby Charlton and another of England's World Cup winners, full-back George Cohen. However, he had only recently celebrated his twentieth birthday and he remained confident of golden days to come.

6
BACK TO THE PINNACLE
1966/67

George Best and Bobby Noble, contemporaries who would experience vividly contrasting fortunes during their Old Trafford tenures.

6
BACK TO THE PINNACLE
1966/67

In 1966, George Best and Bobby Noble were two talented young footballers on the threshold of a season which would end with both of them pocketing League championship medals. They were born within six months of each other and each played prominent roles as Manchester United won the FA Youth Cup in 1964, but while George Best would be sipping champagne with his teammates in the West Ham dressing room after the title had been clinched, poor Bobby Noble was still in the early stages of recovery from an horrendous accident that was to cost him his career and almost claimed his life.

Although they had turned professional at Old Trafford at virtually the same time, and progressed swiftly through the junior ranks together, the slender Belfast boy and the solidly constructed, down-to-earth Mancunian were never particularly close away from the game. However, what they had in common was a nailed-on part in Matt Busby's long-term plans, Best because of his unquestionable genius as an attacker and Noble for his qualities both muscular and constructive at the other end of the pitch, which appeared likely to guarantee him a long-term future as England's left-back. Indeed, when he became dissatisfied with his progress towards a regular first-team place and asked for a transfer, something which in his own heart he never wanted, Busby's unequivocal response spoke volumes of his regard for the rookie defender: 'You'll never leave United as long as I'm here, son!'

Accordingly Noble's breakthrough arrived in 1966/67, and after turning in an efficient performance in a goalless draw at Sunderland in late April 1967, he could reflect that, with only three games of the season to go, his first senior honour – a title gong – was there for the taking. But then, on the final part of his journey home to Sale from Roker Park that evening, Noble suffered grievous head wounds in a car crash for which he was blameless. At first his very survival was in question, but then he rallied and his thoughts turned to reclaiming his place on the ladder to football stardom that had once beckoned so alluringly. He trained as hard as he knew how, but his timing and sharpness had gone, he could no longer anticipate the flight of a ball and his dreams were in ruins. It was a vicious reversal of fortune for the lad whom Busby had chosen to skipper George Best, David Sadler, John Fitzpatrick and the rest in their triumphant Youth Cup campaign, and whom many shrewd judges saw as a future Manchester United captain.

For his part Best, though he spoke little of his contemporary's plight, was deeply moved by the tragedy which had arrived at Noble's door. If anything it strengthened his resolution to live his own life to the full, and that's exactly what he did.

BOBBY NOBLE: *George Best was a brilliant footballer, but in training we always called him a jammy basket. He used to run with the ball, playing it against our legs and getting it back, and at first we thought he was a lucky little so-and-so. But he did it so often that gradually we realised it was deliberate – and that's when we understood just how marvellous a player he was. The fact is, he was a natural. He could go past anybody as if they didn't exist, which as a full-back I found out sooner rather than later. Whichever way the defender tried to tackle, George would dart the other way and he would be gone. Mind, later on he never played against me in training because he knew I'd kick him, and then he wouldn't be able to play on the Saturday. The coaches knew that, too, so after a while they didn't let me loose on him. Usually I ended up being against John Aston, who you could kick all day and he would never flinch. Once I accidentally went over the top in training on Bobby Charlton, and he didn't play in the team at the weekend. I was wearing these big heavy dabs, huge boots which were supposed to strengthen our legs. After that, they kept me away from Bobby, too!*

The time came when George was the best in the world and yet because of his nationality he was unable to play in the World Cup because Northern Ireland didn't qualify, which was a great shame. If he'd been an England player, what an international career he would have had! I've never seen anybody else come up to George. Ryan Giggs has been a terrific ambassador and a wonderful player, but nobody had the magic that Bestie had.

It's amazing to look at archive film of him now. Just start it off in slow motion and then build up gradually to normal speed. His feet were so unbelievably fast that it makes your eyes go funny, and that's just watching him on the screen. Imagine what it was like to face him in real life – absolutely mind-blowing.

When George was playing alongside Denis and Bobby, oh my, that was something. One of them or even two of them could have an off day, but the third one would be likely to win us the game. Coming into a team like that as a young lad was overawing at first. I couldn't believe that I was sitting down to change next to three world-class performers. But I did have my place on merit and around that time people were talking about me as a possible future England left-back, a long-term replacement for Ray Wilson. I wasn't in the side when George won his first League title in 1964/65, but I was there with him when he collected his second in 1966/67, only for a road accident that spring to finish my career when I was just 21. That was a hard pill to swallow.

Bestie and I had signed as apprentices with United in the same year. I was captain of the side which won the FA Youth Cup in 1964, by which time he was already in the first team, already masterful. As a result he played only four times in the boys' competition, both semi-final legs against Manchester City, then the same against Swindon in the final.

Off the pitch, George was a really nice person, very quiet most of the time. I often looked at him and wondered what he was thinking. For all his success, there was never anything boastful about him. I used to pick up Bestie and David Sadler on the way into training because I lived in Cheadle and they were with Mrs Fullaway in Chorlton. In his way, though, I suppose he was a bit of a rum lad, someone who always knew exactly what he wanted to do and went his own way. I didn't used to like ten-pin bowling but he loved it and sometimes after training in the early days we would go to play at a centre near Old Trafford cricket ground. I didn't really fancy it, so more often I did my own thing, usually just having a beer somewhere.

Of course, he liked the girls and they liked him. He was a good-looking boy, after all. Later when we were in the first team it was rare that we socialised together because we had different friends, though once he did take me to a London nightclub after we had played Arsenal. This was in March 1967 and he liked a drink by that stage, although nothing excessive. He was on the spirits; he was never a lager or beer man, like me.

Unfortunately, once George started going downhill the way he did, there was only one way he was going to finish up. It was so very sad because he should have had so many years left in him as a Manchester United man. Often people ask me what he would be like in the modern game, and I tell them he would be virtually unplayable. Life would be so much easier for a dribbler like him, with lighter balls, better pitches and defenders not allowed to tackle from behind – that would be me knackered, *incidentally! Then there is the vastly improved treatment of injuries, new diets and all the benefits of state-of-the-art sports science. I believe that if George Best was playing in 2012, he would be greater than anyone can possibly imagine.*

▼ One of the key influences on George Best's life during his time with Manchester United was his landlady, Mrs Fullaway, who was nonplussed the first time she laid eyes on him, believing he was far too scrawny to become a professional footballer. Although she was shrewd in almost every other way, she got that one wrong, and George spent around a decade, on and off, living in her council house in Chorlton-cum-Hardy, Manchester, which became a much-needed haven for him. In fact, after overcoming the initial difficulty of barely understanding a word he uttered because of his broad Belfast accent, she played a telling role in his rise, making sure he ate properly and dispensing plenty of sound advice, not all of which was heeded. For his part, George always thought the world of Mrs Fullaway, who became something akin to a surrogate mother to the United star at a time when such a homely, stable figure was sorely needed in his life.

Manchester United's head groundsman in the 1960s and for many years before, local man Joe Royle, hugs Denis Law and George Best for the camera in front of the south stand at Old Trafford. It was a rare moment in the limelight for the diminutive Mancunian, who was a warm, delightfully unassuming character with whom most of the players loved to pass the time of day, George particularly relishing Joe's tales of characters from long ago.

For all that he was quiet and modest, Manchester United's head groundsman was not slow to show his disapproval if anyone, and that included the players, should dare to trespass on to his sacred turf for anything but a match or a scheduled practice session. During an era when the drainage was notably poorer than it is today, Joe – whose brother, Dave, looked after the club's training ground at The Cliff, in Broughton – needed to be fiercely protective of the Old Trafford surface if he was to prevent it becoming a quagmire for much of the season.

In 1966/67, the Royle expertise was put to productive use as United were crowned champions for the second time in three seasons, with nobody gracing that hallowed patch of grass more enchantingly than George Best. Having recovered largely if never quite completely from his springtime knee surgery, the Irishman was an ever-present in the League campaign for the only time in his 11 seasons in the first team, scoring ten goals and setting up countless opportunities for the likes of Denis (23 strikes), David Herd (16) and Bobby Charlton (12).

Just lie back and think of United, young man. So relentlessly did opposing defenders hunt down George Best that trainer Jack Crompton was frequently called on to brandish his dripping sponge, a bracing treatment that was hardly at the cutting edge of medical science but which could usually be relied upon to revive a stricken footballer.

Opponents who believed they could intimidate George Best invariably had another think coming. For all his waif-like build, the nimble attacker could tackle like a runaway plough. Those slender limbs were remarkably resilient and, no matter how much punishment he took, he would bounce back for more. He saw losing the ball, even by foul means, as a personal insult and he was blessed with an exceptionally high pain threshold. Thus unless he was practically a hospital case he would be out for retribution in the most effective way possible – by fighting to regain possession and then hurting the opposition with his astonishing skill.

Jack Crompton was the goalkeeper in Matt Busby's FA Cup-winning team of 1948, which finished as runners-up in four of the first five title races after the war. He was a fitness fanatic and firmly of the old school of spongemen, who expected players to deal with their pain like men. In George Best, he was not disappointed.

JACK CROMPTON: *I found George to be a nice, straightforward, honest lad. He never caused me the slightest problem. At least, once you got him to the ground he was fine. Sometimes it might be a bit of a job finding him!*

There was always something about playing Chelsea, particularly at Stamford Bridge, so close to the glamour and the glitz of the King's Road that he so relished, that brought out the showman in George Best. Certainly he gave many of his most luminous performances at the Blues' west London home, notably on his first appearance there in 1964 when he received an ovation from fans and fellow footballers alike. He was equally irresistible on a rainy November afternoon in 1966 when United, once again on the road to the title, prevailed by three goals to one.

The bare mechanics of the game can be dealt with swiftly. Chelsea's generally excellent keeper Peter Bonetti spilled a howitzer from Paddy Crerand, which allowed John Aston to pop in the opener two minutes before the interval; Best made it 2–0 shortly after the hour-mark; Hollins pulled one back for the hosts with a speculative 30-yarder that crept past United custodian Alex Stepney via an upright; then Best set up the final goal for Aston a quarter of an hour from the end.

But while such details have receded with the passing of time, what lingers indelibly in the memory, as vivid as the rockets which soared above the capital later on that Guy Fawkes night, was the masterpiece that was George's goal and the manner in which he toyed repeatedly with the wretched Chelsea rearguard.

Tortured more devilishly than most was Chelsea's number three, Eddie McCreadie, who repeatedly found himself lunging unavailingly in the wizard's wake (top right). Even when fouled and seemingly off balance George would somehow stretch to poke the ball beyond the challenge of yet another would-be marker (bottom right).

The infernal dilemma facing the men in blue was captured beautifully by Albert Barham in the *Guardian*:

Does one really seek to up-end Best as often as possible, as Eddie McCreadie tried to on Saturday? Such a policy, when it fails, makes the full-back appear rather foolish, lying on the ground as the skimpy figure, black locks billowing, skips away to create more havoc. Or does one stand off, watchful and ready? McCreadie tried that, too, and lost out. He stood, head thrust forward, glaring, poised to pounce. Best out-thought him, flicked the ball sideways with his left foot to David Sadler, bounded forward, and was lost to McCreadie. Back came the precise pass and Best, denying himself the pleasure of a second to steady himself, though he had created time enough and space, shot and beat Bonetti for the finest goal of the match [below].

An alternative, but equally lyrical account, was offered by Ken Jones in the *Daily Mirror*:

It was one of those moments that not even the tricks of memory can polish into something more marvellous. It was there to see, to savour, to enthuse over – the genius of George Best, Manchester United's Irish international. For seconds that must have seemed an age to Chelsea full-back Eddie McCreadie, he was still, his body keeled over at an incredible angle, his right foot poised like a wand over the ball. Then Best was away, sprinting for a return to the pass he had stabbed to the feet of David Sadler. An incredible shot, hit off the wrong foot, swept past a bewildered Peter Bonetti and

a capacity crowd at Stamford Bridge were suddenly living lavishly with the greatness of it all. It was more than just a great goal. It was absolute proof that in the ultimate it is the magic of the individual that makes the game live.

▲ George Best shivers the Scoreboard End crossbar with his first-ever penalty for Manchester United as Liverpool's Scottish international goalkeeper Tommy Lawrence plunges to his left at a momentarily hushed Old Trafford in December 1966. A split-second later all but the visitors' section of the ground erupted in a tumultuous roar to greet the Irishman's second goal of the contest as the ball bounced over the line, thus giving Matt Busby's side a 2–1 advantage after half an hour. Sadly for the hosts, the reigning champions equalised on the stroke of half-time as another Scotland star, Ian St John, completed his own brace.

Curiously, in view of the passionate entreaties of coaches everywhere for all players to be on their toes in such a situation, just in case of a rebound from the woodwork or the keeper, here everyone but the two principal protagonists are flat-footed, seemingly resigned to the outcome. Bobby Charlton, on the left with hands on hips, clearly has a touching faith in the fiercely determined George's prowess from the spot, while among the Merseyside spectators are Bobby's fellow World Cup winner Roger Hunt (slightly left of centre, in similar pose), Chris Lawler, Ian Callaghan and Tommy Smith.

Best had been handed the responsibility because United's regular penalty marksman, Denis Law, was absent with injury, as was the key defender Nobby Stiles. In such circumstances, a 2–2 draw wasn't a bad result for the home team on an afternoon of tempestuous action. Ron Yeats, Liverpool's man-mountain of a centre-half, committed the foul on Jim Ryan – standing in for Law – to concede the spot-kick, and was also involved in an incident which saw the booking of Best in an era when referees were exceedingly slow to hand out an official caution. George had pushed the Aberdonian colossus in the chest and Yeats, at least in the unanimous opinion of the United contingent, had over-reacted, which persuaded the official to step in. It was typical of the United man not to be intimidated by a fellow standing half a foot taller than him, but no grudges were held after the final whistle had gone. Despite the rivalry of the two clubs' fans, which would reach sickeningly unhealthy levels in the decades ahead, many of the United and Liverpool footballers were close friends with each other, as were the two bosses, Busby and the gleefully irascible, often wickedly funny Bill Shankly.

BILL FOULKES: *I was lucky enough to play with so many wonderful players during my time with Manchester United, and the most amazing of them all was George Best. In my humble opinion, he was the most astonishing raw talent the game has ever known. Yes, I'd put him up there with Pelé, Maradona, di Stefano, Cruyff or anybody else under the sun. We felt we had the makings of a top team already, but then George appeared and kicked us into an entirely different dimension.*

His footballing make-up was practically flawless and I believe he could have excelled in any position. Then there was the fact, which nobody liked to admit, that when George was dribbling on his merry way, the rest of us could take a bit of a breather, and as the years went by, some of us needed that rather more than others . . .

▶ Tottenham Hotspur's Mike England holds his arms wide to indicate that he has not impeded George Best unfairly as the red-shirted imp shimmies past on his beguiling way to creating more mayhem in the north Londoners' rearguard. The big Welshman, one of the finest defenders in the land and a man coveted by Matt Busby during his earlier days at Blackburn Rovers, might as well be shrugging his shoulders in a gesture of helplessness. When George Best was truly in the mood, there was little any opponent could do to curb him.

◄ Lapping a snowy Old Trafford in training alongside David Sadler, one of his closest friends at the club, George Best might not have been relishing the monotonous exercise – he always preferred to have a football at his feet – but he would have been ready to keep running as long as trainer Jack Crompton decreed. Certainly at this point in his career, no matter how potentially draining his recent social activities might have been, George was a fastidious performer of training tasks, always at or near the front of the pack when it came to races. Jack was something of a martinet when it came to ensuring that his charges put in the hard yards, and he deserves his share of the plaudits which went United's way as they lifted a succession of major trophies in the 1960s.

DAVID SADLER: *George was born to play football, and he was a great trainer. I'm doing well to keep up with him here! His principal strength as a player was that he didn't have a weakness. There was a time when he could have played anywhere in the team and been the best in that position. It sounds incredible, but towards the end of the 1960s he could do everything better than everybody else.*

Dancing with characteristically nimble grace in the Upton Park sunlight on the afternoon the League title was clinched, George Best attempts to demonstrate his craft as a persuasive dummy salesman, and West Ham defender Paul Heffer seems about to dive in for a purchase. Meanwhile Denis Law darts into space just in case a pass comes his way, surely an example of hope exceeding expectation.

George Best (ironically in light of later events, the only man without a drink in his hand) is at the back next to his chum David Sadler. Lining up at the front are, left to right, Denis Law, John Aston, Shay Brennan, Bill Foulkes, Tony Dunne, Paddy Crerand, Nobby Stiles and Bobby Charlton. It's rather a shame that the one man missing from the photograph is goalkeeper Alex Stepney, who had proved a massive influence after being bought from Chelsea by Matt Busby in the previous autumn. Indeed, the United boss even went on record as saying that Stepney's reliability had been the difference between winning and losing the championship.

On a diamond-bright East London afternoon in May 1967, the penultimate Saturday of the League campaign, Manchester United had merely to do better than their nearest rivals, Nottingham Forest, in a simultaneous match to claim their second crown in three years. In the event they brushed aside the Hammers – including England's World Cup-winning trio of ten months earlier, Bobby Moore, Geoff Hurst and Martin Peters – with majestic ease, handing out a 6–1 drubbing while Forest slumped to anti-climactic defeat at Southampton.

In truth it was all over after ten minutes, by which time Bobby Charlton, Paddy Crerand and Bill Foulkes had put the visitors three goals to the good. Indeed, so runaway was United's success that Matt Busby, who had made stately rather than sprightly progress from the away dressing room to the side of the pitch, missed Bobby's second-minute opener, and it wasn't until half-time that the manager of the champions-elect discovered the true score.

By then George had added another on 25 minutes after bamboozling West Ham full-back John Charles, and although the defender reduced the deficit straight after the interval, he then conceded a penalty which was converted by Denis Law before the Scot completed the scoring with 11 minutes left to play.

Sadly the day was marred by disgraceful scenes of fighting on the terraces, before, during and after the match, with combatants being led away with blood pouring from head wounds. During the season United supporters had been involved in too many disturbances, and that became a worrying trend.

But although there might have been fighting in the streets around the Boleyn Ground, all was sweetness and light in the dressing room as Manchester United celebrated their title triumph. As for George Best, although he was still experiencing twinges from his knee surgery of a year earlier, his star, and his influence, continued to rise, along with his self-belief. Busby declared that Best had more confidence in his own ability than he had seen in any other sportsman, a view with which his enthusiastic lieutenant, Jimmy Murphy, concurred heartily: 'Confidence is the key, and he has it in bucket-loads. I reckon if it were possible for him to play in a forward line which also included Di Stefano, Puskas, Pelé and Eusebio, his attitude would be – and now watch George Best of Northern Ireland play!' George wouldn't celebrate his twenty-first birthday until later that month, and the sporting world was at his twinkling feet.

7

GOALSCORER-IN-CHIEF

1967/68

7
GOALSCORER-IN-CHIEF
1967/68

George Best became more important than ever before to Manchester United in 1967/68. With Denis Law suffering serial knee trouble, and missing more matches than at any previous time since his own arrival at Old Trafford in 1962, Matt Busby needed a new goalscorer-in-chief, and it was to the Irishman that he turned.

The summons was answered in glorious fashion, despite George having some cartilage issues of his own, albeit at nowhere near the level that was plaguing Denis. The highest Best goal tally to date had been 16 in 1965/66. This time, given even more freedom to roam than ever and spending much of his time in central positions, he doubled that total to 32 in the major competitions, 28 of them in the League. It was to be the most prolific campaign of his career, and it so very nearly carried the Red Devils to the hitherto unattained double of the First Division championship and the European Cup.

With Law ailing and the prolific but ageing spearhead David Herd never quite regaining his former sharpness following a broken leg, Matt Busby had turned his thoughts to possible outside replacements, with such eminent names being mentioned as England World Cup hero Geoff Hurst of West Ham, Chelsea's prolific Bobby Tambling, the pacy and clever Peter Dobing of Stoke City, and Scottish international Jim McCalliog, who had been cutting a dash for Sheffield Wednesday. There were even rumours about signing the mesmerically tricky Jimmy Johnstone from Celtic, only a few months after he had helped Celtic become the first British team to lift the European Cup by overturning AC Milan in Lisbon. If the wee ginger wingman had joined United, then presumably George would have switched to a central position, and when Law had recovered then Busby would have been able to boast a phenomenal attack including George, Jimmy, Denis and Bobby Charlton, a prospect to set the Stretford Enders drooling.

As it was Busby relied on his own historically successful production line for a key

Clad in the V-necked summer-weight shirt Manchester United adopted briefly at the outset of the new campaign, George Best delivers a right-footed cross against Leicester City at Old Trafford in August. In front of more than 51,000 fans, the Red Devils could only draw 1–1 with their visitors – and that courtesy of a rare goal from centre-half Bill Foulkes – to continue a fitful start to the season which had encompassed an opening-day defeat at Everton followed by a home victory against Leeds United.

reinforcement, promoting young Brian Kidd to regular first-team duty. The tall curly-haired teenager from Collyhurst, a suburb of north Manchester, made an early impact on the close-season tour of Australia, then shone once more in the curtain-raiser to the new campaign, an entertaining FA Charity Shield clash with FA Cup winners Tottenham Hotspur at Old Trafford. That game finished 3–3, and for once that season George Best was thoroughly overshadowed by two unforgettable incidents.

His Northern Ireland teammate Pat Jennings, the Spurs goalkeeper, riveted the attention after only five minutes by scoring with a gigantic drop-kick, which bounced in front of the United custodian Alex Stepney before sailing over his head into the net. That put the visitors two in front, but Bobby Charlton had levelled matters within a quarter of an hour, and his second goal was sensational even by Old Trafford standards. Law, not fully fit but sprightly enough on this rainy August afternoon, received the ball in the left-back position – what he was doing there was something of a mystery – and uncharacteristically set off on a mazy Best-like run past several defenders before knocking the ball out to Kidd, who was darting in from the left touchline. Showing the awareness of a veteran, the boy rolled the ball into the path of the charging Charlton, who thumped it with thunderous power from 25 yards. It smacked the net above and behind the flailing Jennings, who had leapt like a salmon in pursuit of the hurtling leather, but to no avail.

With Best in typically beguiling form, the rest of the afternoon unfolded entertainingly, with Law grabbing another equaliser near the end and the teams sharing the trophy. As an appetiser of the drama that was to follow over the next ten months, that contest would have taken some beating.

There were pundits who reckoned that, having won the League championship for the second time in three seasons, Matt Busby needed to make root-and-branch changes to his team if they were going to push on towards his ultimate goal, the European Cup. They pointed out that, having peaked so brilliantly in the 1966 semi-final against Benfica, they had slumped dismally when faced with dour, physical opponents in Partizan Belgrade at the semi-final stage.

However, such critics were in the minority and Busby chose to disagree. He main-

▶ Slim but whippily resilient, eyes constantly glued to the ball, often crouching but always perfectly balanced and ready to dart away in the opposite direction the moment an opponent committed himself to a challenge, George Best was reminiscent, in some ways, of the great Sir Stanley Matthews, the seemingly ageless genius who had showcased his extraordinary talents on the football grounds of England for some three decades. But between the two great players there were a couple of major sporting differences. Like the Stoke City and Blackpool icon, George created countless scoring opportunities for his teammates, but unlike the older man, he also scored heavily himself. On the other hand, the incredible Sir Stan was still playing League football into his second half-century, while the mercurial Irishman was a mere 27 years old when he made his farewell appearance for Manchester United. You pays your money and you takes your choice!

tained that only Foulkes could be termed a true veteran, and the rugged ex-miner was such a fitness fanatic that the evidence of his birth certificate was rendered irrelevant. Of the rest, only full-back Shay Brennan had turned 30 and he was now having to fight for his place with the talented young Scot Francis Burns. True, there were long-term fitness worries over frontman Denis Law and Nobby Stiles, such a combative and intelligent presence alongside Foulkes in the centre of defence, but Busby believed the influential pair could be nursed back to full health. Thus, despite his despair when United had failed at the penultimate hurdle in '66, he was quietly confident as he led his troops into his fourth European Cup campaign. In each of the previous three they had reached the last four. Now it was time to do even better, and in the 21-year-old George Best, he reckoned he possessed the trump card . . .

In an almost uncanny echo of the modern era, in 1967 Manchester City were emerging as a genuine threat to their erstwhile dominators from Old Trafford. Revolutionised by the inspirational, enlightened management duo of Joe Mercer and Malcolm Allison, City had risen from the Second Division in 1966, consolidated steadily during the following term and now were admirably equipped for a tilt at wresting the title from United's grasp.

Watched by Denis Law and the temporarily moustachioed George Best, the third member of the glorious trinity, Bobby Charlton, notches one of his two goals with which the reigning Reds beat the resurgent Blues 2–1 at Maine Road in September 1967. The City men, unable to intervene, are (left to right) Colin Bell, Glyn Pardoe, Mike Doyle and skipper Tony Book.

At that time United fans were confident of retaining their crown, perceiving that the principal opposition was likely to emanate either from Liverpool or Leeds, or maybe Everton, but they were to prove sorely mistaken. Although this victory saw Busby's side leapfrog his old chum Mercer's, leading them by a point with a game in hand, City had the benefit of not being distracted by European competition and proved to possess stamina aplenty, even after falling five points adrift of their illustrious neighbours by the turn of the year.

They had assembled a formidable attacking line-up, comprising Mike Summerbee, Colin Bell, Francis Lee, the oft-undersung Neil Young and the combative Tony Coleman, while in Alan Oakes, George Heslop and the United-loathing Mike Doyle they had a half-back line the equal of any in division. Full-backs Tony Book and Glyn Pardoe were both stern and creative in turn and Ken Mulhearn, between the posts, was a solid citizen. Still the majority of the Old Trafford faithful were scornful of City's championship credentials, but a rude awakening was in the offing.

Liverpool however, now there was a team to be taken seriously, Bill Shankly's men having won the title in both 1963/64 and 1965/66, alternating with United as the First Division top dogs throughout the decade's middle years. Thus the 2–1 victory at Anfield in November, which shattered the Merseysiders' proud 100 per cent home record, was greeted rapturously by the vocal Manchester contingent of supporters that had travelled 30 miles west along the East Lancs Road for the crucial contest.

George Best was the star of the show for the visitors, putting them in front with an exquisitely judged glancing header from John Aston's cross after 18 minutes, then doubling the lead by nudging the ball beyond Liverpool keeper Tommy Lawrence (right), having escaped the close attentions of big Ron Yeats, the towering centre-half in the middle of the picture. Roger Hunt, one of England's World Cup heroes two years earlier, set up a tense finale by reducing the deficit with seven minutes left on the clock, but United held out to claim two points that saw them overtake their hosts in the league table. In the final reckoning, though, it wasn't Liverpool that United had to worry about after all.

▼ There was no mercy on offer for an old friend and adversary, Graham Williams of West Bromwich Albion, when the Baggies came calling at Old Trafford in December 1967. The doggedly determined Welsh international full-back, who had been George Best's first marker when he had made his senior debut for United on the same turf more than four years earlier, once again had the unenviable task of shackling the Irishman but, as with this awkward tackle, he found little joy in the assignment.

Though Williams battled manfully all afternoon, and high-flying Albion proved to be among the most entertaining visitors of the whole campaign, George scored both goals in a 2–1 United triumph in front of prime minister Harold Wilson, among 52,896 others. First he netted with a shot from an acutely narrow angle midway through the first period, then he dispatched a John Aston corner with an emphatic header. The Baggies bounced back through a John Kaye strike a quarter of an hour from the end, but late pressure didn't produce an equaliser, although the bustling marksman Jeff Astle went perilously close.

▲ George Best loved to employ his trickery against the most illustrious opponents available, so he truly relished this contest with England and West Ham skipper Bobby Moore, the darling of the southern-based press, in January 1968. Not that there was any lack of respect for the serene and supremely talented 'Mooro', who appears to have lunged prematurely here, enabling the United man to nick the ball to one side before accelerating unimpeded into the Hammers' penalty box. Matt Busby's men went on to win 3–1, with Bobby Charlton, George himself (with a header) and the unobtrusive but efficient John Aston supplying the goals.

At this point United were nearing the end of a 12-match unbeaten run in the League, and they were piping-hot favourites to retain their title, which would have made them champions in three years out of four. But all too soon they would fall prey to chronic inconsistency, with significant injuries to half the team – Denis Law, Bill Foulkes, Nobby

Stiles, Tony Dunne and Brian Kidd – playing their part in a decline which encompassed seven defeats in their last 15 games. As for George, he appeared to revel in the extra responsibility which was placed on his narrow shoulders, sometimes appearing to take on an opposing defence on his own.

◄ For all his dazzling brilliance with the ball at his feet, and his unfathomable ability to confound virtually any marker in the world, George Best was not fundamentally inclined to taunt an opponent. He was, and always remained, a sportsman who relished the contest, but was never inclined to rub in his obvious superiority in the skill stakes – unless, that is, he was serially provoked. Of course, that did happen, as in this clash with Sheffield Wednesday, in which he is beckoning wing-half Gerry Young (out of shot) to 'come and get it' with an arrogance that was simply not typical. A puzzling aspect is that the once-capped England international Young, though a formidable adversary, was firmly of the 'hard but fair' school and it seems unlikely that he had been kicking George all over the park

prior to this moment. It seems certain, though, that Best had been repeatedly assailed by somebody, and was therefore at the end of his tether. It's possible that Young was the victim of mistaken identity, or perhaps the Irishman was simply in a bad mood. Whatever the answer, this is a classic image, one of the most evocative ever created of the inimitable George Best.

▲ There was simply no limit to George Best's inventiveness, no end to his sleight of foot, as Tottenham Hotspur defender Phil Beal discovered in a typically exhilarating encounter between Bill Nicholson's North Londoners and the Red Devils at White Hart Lane in February 1968. This was a backheel of which Socrates – the imperious, somewhat eccentric Brazilian midfielder, who died in 2011 and who had specialised in such deft manoeuvres – would have been proud.

It was representative of a relentlessly thrilling contest, in which Spurs had taken the lead after only two minutes through a goal by England centre-forward Martin Chivers, who had looked to be in an offside position. That gave United plenty of time to fight back, however, and Best, at his most magical, led the way. After 18 minutes, though surrounded by five Tottenham defenders in the Tottenham box, he managed to steer the ball past his countryman and friend Pat Jennings for a deserved equaliser. Next he earned a penalty when he was brought down by Cyril Knowles, only for Bobby Charlton – given the job in the absence of Denis Law – to fail from the spot.

However, Bobby made spectacular amends with only two minutes left, running half the length of the pitch to score an unforgettable winner. Thanks to a third-round FA Cup meeting, which Spurs had won after a replay, this was the third time the two sides had met in the space of a week. During the season they clashed on five occasions, twice each in the First Division and the FA Cup and once in the Charity Shield. United shaded the series, with two wins, two draws and a defeat.

▶ Though below average height and slim with it, George Best was a ferocious competitor in the air, willing to mix it with the biggest and most muscular of opponents, in this instance Mike England, Tottenham Hotspur's Welsh international centre-half. The Irishman scored plenty of goals with his head, too, the product not only of courage and athleticism, but also of timing. George was able to discern the arc of a cross with remarkable accuracy, which usually ensured that he met the ball at the top of his leap. With such pinpoint deliverers as Paddy Crerand, Bobby Charlton and John Aston in the United side – and in earlier days John Connelly came firmly into that category, too – he was well supplied with ammunition. Still, though, it never seemed less than astonishing to see his dark head climbing above a posse of six-footers, and often a split second later the ball would have flashed into the net.

For all his myriad attributes, however, George and his teammates were powerless to prevent the League title of 1967/68 slipping away to their local adversaries. On the Saturday morning of 27 April, United led City by four points, with the Reds having three games to play, the Blues four. That fateful day Matt Busby's men, shorn of defenders Shay Brennan and Bill Foulkes through injury and with the talisman Denis Law far from fully fit, went down to a shock 6–3 reverse at West Bromwich, while City were scraping a 1–0 victory over Sheffield Wednesday, courtesy of a freakish own goal. Two days later Joe Mercer's side beat Everton at Maine Road to wipe out United's lead, and with City having a better goal average – the archaic predecessor to goal difference for splitting clubs on the same number of points – the advantage had passed to the Blues.

On 4 May George strove mightily to redress the balance, striking a hat-trick in a 6–0 home defeat of Newcastle, but with Mike Summerbee netting in City's crucial 3–1 win at Tottenham, United were still the underdogs on the final day of the League programme.

On paper, though, they had the easier task, facing Sunderland at Old Trafford while City made the trip to Newcastle. Both north-eastern clubs were mired in mid-table and had little to play for, but while the Wearsiders excelled themselves with a 2–1 triumph over a United eleven that might just have had its eyes on the forthcoming European Cup final, the Magpies proved easy pickings for City, Summerbee again making the scoresheet in a thrilling 4–3 victory at St James' Park.

Thus the championship passed from Old Trafford to Maine Road, Matt Busby magnanimously shook his old pal Joe Mercer's hand in congratulation, and relations between the two sets of players remained generally cordial. Such was the atmosphere of top-level professional football in 1968.

George Best with his parents, Annie and Dickie, in October 1967, in the fish and chip restaurant he bought for them in Belfast. At that stage of his life, he returned frequently to his boyhood home. For all the glamour and the glory that had come to his door, he always remained devoted to his mum and dad and his five siblings, sisters Carol, Barbara, Grace and Julie, and brother Ian.

▶ One of George Best's most implacable rivals throughout his Old Trafford heyday was Ron Harris of Chelsea, nicknamed 'Chopper' for reasons obvious to anyone who had witnessed the abrasive Londoner at his work. But for all his lurid image as a monstrously formidable destroyer, Harris was an intelligent reader of the game and often timed his tackles to perfection. Of course if, having taken the ball, he then followed through to take the man, thus offering a chilling

warning to his victim, then so much the better as far as Chopper was concerned.

However, in George he faced a serial tormentor whom he could never intimidate. For all his slender build, the Irishman was like a streak of weathered whipcord, immutably tough, often rolling with challenges that would have snapped less hardy individuals in two, psychologically speaking at least. If he did go down, then 49 times out of 50 he would be back on his feet in the blink of an eye, endlessly defiant and ready to re-enter the fray.

8

LIVING THE ULTIMATE DREAM
SPRINGTIME 1968

8
LIVING THE
ULTIMATE DREAM
SPRINGTIME 1968

Though Manchester United stumbled disastrously in pursuit of a third League title in four seasons, they proved less fallible on the road to European glory. One of the key contributions was this goal, plundered sensationally by George Best. It might be termed the second most important hit of his career, and without it he might never have had the opportunity to light up Wembley with his most famous strike of all. A savage left-foot drive against Real Madrid at Old Trafford (opposite) gave the Red Devils a desperately needed, if fearfully slender, first-leg lead against Real Madrid in the semi-final of the European Cup in April 1968.

The breakthrough came ten minutes before the interval of a tense first half when Brian Kidd freed John Aston to break away on the left flank of United's attack. The winger took the ball in his stride, pulled back a low cross from near the byline and Best, who had found space some 15 yards out, met the rolling leather as sweetly as any pulverising cover-drive from the flashing bat of Clive Lloyd, who was just moving in along the Warwick Road to become the new idol at cricket's version of the Theatre of Dreams. The missile rocketed high into the net, with startled Spanish keeper Antonio Betancort helpless to interrupt its thrilling passage.

That was the only goal of the game, and afterwards aficionados of continental football proclaimed that United had not done enough to go through. But before revisiting the drama of the second leg at the Bernabeu Stadium, it is worth remembering how hard United and George Best, who didn't miss a match in the competition, worked to reach the later stages.

The trail commenced in less than exacting circumstances, an Old Trafford encounter with Hibernians of Malta – a team of part-timers coached by a priest, Father Hilary Tagliaferro – offering no problems. In fact, the Maltese battled gamely, and though they lost 4–0 – with Denis Law and David Sadler both scoring twice – they warned that the Reds

would face a much more taxing task on the rolled sand, gravel and lime that constituted the surface at the Gzira Stadium. So it proved as United took a safety-first attitude in the scorching heat, playing out a goalless draw which was an immense disappointment to their vast army of Maltese supporters, who had bought tickets in the expectation of seeing a buccaneering attacking display by their Old Trafford heroes. Still, George Best and company were feted like royalty, festooned with flowers and loaded with gifts, which was more than a little embarrassing, all things considered.

Certainly the good-natured Hibs stood in stark contrast to United's next opponents, the Yugoslavian champions Sarajevo, who took their name from the town in which the assassination of Archduke Ferdinand had sparked the First World War. Once the first leg started in Sarajevo, somehow such a violent association seemed wholly understandable, as the hosts subjected United to a sustained physical assault and, not surprisingly, Best was particularly a target, finding himself on the end of some horrifically dangerous challenges. However, like his sometimes combustible teammate Paddy Crerand, he retained his composure admirably, though Paddy Crerand was moved to remark afterwards: 'Our trainer Jack Crompton was on the field so often that the fans must have thought he was playing!'

United were happy to emerge from the Yugoslavian battle-zone with a 0–0 draw, only to find their opponents almost equally combative in the return leg at Old Trafford. The deadlock was broken early on, when Aston nudged home after a powerful Best header had been palmed out by keeper Muftic, but at that point Sarajevo remained relatively restrained. That changed in the second half after George had lashed out unwisely in retaliation for a cynical foul and Muftic feigned serious hurt. As a result Fahrudin Prljaca embarked on a revenge assault, kicking the Irishman so openly that the referee had no alternative but to send the offender from the field. Thereafter Sarajevo's composure evaporated altogether, their defenders more intent on kicking opponents than the ball, and their disarray allowed Best to make it 2–0 after 65 minutes. A late strike by Salih Delalic proved scant consolation for the visitors, who were left to wonder what they might have achieved if they had concentrated on playing football from the start.

That hard-won victory was enough to earn United a place in the quarter-finals, where they met a very different kind of opposition. Indeed, the Polish side Gornik Zabrze performed with such a nobly sporting attitude that George and his teammates lined up by the tunnel to clap them off after the first leg at Old Trafford. The fact that United had collected a 2–0 lead might have had something to do with the expression of such finer feelings, but Matt Busby's men were genuinely impressed by Gornik's Corinthian approach.

In fact, it had been a notably close contest, with Best being held effectively by his determined and efficient marker Henryk Latocha. Until the hour mark, that is, when George finally wriggled away and lashed in a shot which Florenski could only turn into his own net. After that, with play-maker Crerand in magisterial form, United dominated but were repeatedly frustrated by the brilliance of Kostka between the Polish sticks until the last minute, when Brian Kidd scrambled a much-needed second goal.

That made the trip to the snowy wastes of Silesia for the second leg a little less daunting, but still it was to prove a deeply uncomfortable experience. Playing on packed ice in a stop–start blizzard was hardly conducive to flowing football but the Reds –

An ecstatic George Best turns on the dressing room shower at the Bernabeu Stadium after Manchester United have picked themselves up off the floor to beat Real Madrid and thus moved within touching distance of Matt Busby's holy grail, the European Cup.

fortified by the presence of Best's old youth-team chum, the steely John Fitzpatrick, in anticipation of a hard game – rose to the occasion, concentrating fiercely from first whistle to last. Even George, with his phenomenal natural balance, found it difficult to keep his feet on the treacherous surface, but although United never really looked like adding to their score, they limited Gornik to a single goal from their world-class marksman Wlodek Lubanksi. Thus although the Red Devils lost 1–0 on that frozen night behind the Iron Curtain, they prevailed 2–1 on aggregate and had preserved the club's proud record of having reached the semi-finals of the European Cup on every occasion they had entered club football's premier competition. But, as George Best declared through chattering teeth as United left the Ernest Pohl Stadium, now it was time for the hard part.

And so it was back to Old Trafford and that desperately narrow victory over the Spanish champions, Real Madrid, courtesy of Best's thumping finish. Unsurprisingly, the Irishman also played a central role in the second leg at the Bernabeu, as the Red Devils were forced to fight back from 3–2 down at the interval to level the scores on the night, thus winning the overall tie 4–3.

Matt Busby's men had looked a truly disheartened bunch as they trooped off the pitch after the first 45 minutes. With Real having scored three times, and with United replying only through a chronic miskick by Zoco which had spun into his own net, the home fans and players alike were gleeful at the interval, clearly believing the game was as good as over. But Busby hadn't become one of the top bosses in the history of the game for nothing, and he repeatedly reminded his men that they were only 3–2 behind on aggregate, pointing out that one goal could puncture the Spaniards' self-belief, which was now bordering on complacency.

He abandoned the uncharacteristically cautious tactics he had employed in the first period, declaring: 'We're Manchester United, let's have a go at them.' It was a psychological masterstroke, not least because the players loved this ageing Scotsman dearly and they yearned to give him his heart's desire.

Thus there was a new light of battle in the Red Devils' eyes as they ran back out in front of a baying 126,000-strong multitude, and a fresh snappiness about all their work, not least the close physical attention handed out by defensive dreadnought Nobby Stiles to Madrid's star man, Amancio. Gradually the realisation that they were not in for a cakewalk dawned on the men in all-white, but time ticked on relentlessly, until only 15 minutes remained and the Mancunian supporters on the Bernabeu's vast terracing were fearing the worst. But the fire still burned brightly in the belly of Paddy Crerand, who lofted a free-kick into the Madrid box, Bill Foulkes managed to knock it on and somehow David Sadler nudged the ball over the line. It was perhaps the messiest, most nondescript goal of Sadler's career, but certainly it was the most important, because now Real's hitherto buoyant confidence just shrank and died. The preening and the showboating stopped, to be replaced by haunting uncertainty, the realisation that they had a massive job still to do and that a brigade of ferociously motivated red-shirted demons stood in their path.

The stage was set perfectly for George Best, and he did not disappoint. Crerand took a long throw down the right touchline and the Irishman ran on to it, then squirmed past Sanchis and Zoco to reach the byline before peering into the centre to see who might be there to receive a pass. His best bet was Brian Kidd or Bobby Charlton, or maybe John Aston or Sadler had made the requisite surge. But no, pounding into view was none other than Big Bill, the normally impassive streak of granite who rarely ventured out of his own half and had mustered only eight goals in 682 games for the club. In that crucial split second, if George had had time to think, he might have pondered on Bill's lack of qualification as a goal hero, then taken a shot himself or jockeyed for position to find another teammate, one who was on nodding acquaintance, at least, with the art of placing ball into net. But instinct took over and he rolled a perfect delivery to the feet of Foulkes and, miracle of miracles, he popped it into the bottom corner with all the aplomb of any specialist marksman who had ever graced the game.

If Real had slumped at David's equaliser, they positively withered in the face of Bill's bombshell, and thereafter United retained their discipline to see out the last 12 minutes. Back in the dressing room, where Best and Sadler frolicked in the shower in their full kit, Busby and Charlton were crying in each other's arms. The long and painful road on which they had set out a dozen years earlier had led them, at last, to the final of the European Cup.

BILL FOULKES: *Manchester United's winner in the European Cup semi-final against Real Madrid in the Bernabeu was the stuff of sheer fantasy. I could never have dreamed that I would combine with George Best to see us through to the final at Wembley. Had it been Bobby or Denis involved with George, or maybe Brian Kidd or Paddy Crerand, it would have been a bit more believable. How on earth could the team's granddad, who had only managed to find the scoresheet eight times in nearly 700 games spread over a decade and a half, be on hand to slot home one of the most important goals in the club's history? Mind you, I must admit that the little Irish genius served it up to me on a plate.*

United got a throw-in on halfway and, although I was not in the habit of piling forward, now something prompted me to advance. I said to my defensive partner Nobby Stiles, who was far more likely than me to get in the opposition's half: 'Stay here, I'm going up.' Understandably enough, he asked me what in the hell I was doing, but I didn't hang around for a debate.

I showed for the ball but Paddy, doubtlessly unable to believe his own eyes, threw it to George. Now Bestie went down the right touchline, dancing past several tackles in his typical fashion, and I kept going, too. Eventually, when he looked up, I was the only United player in the box. My first thought was that he would never pass to me – who could blame him? – and that he would try to score at the near post.

But as he feinted one way, wrong-footing the Real defenders, I read what was in his mind. I had seen him do it so often, albeit with Denis or Bobby or David Herd in the middle instead of me. So I took three steps back and, sure enough, he rolled it perfectly into my path. All I had to do was sidefoot it into the net.

It all seemed unreal, like I was frozen in time. When everyone came to congratulate me the first thing I did was to tell Nobby to stay back because there were still 15 minutes to go. He called me a miserable bugger and clearly George wondered why I wasn't showing any emotion. But I saved that for later. All that mattered to me in that moment was that, having yanked ourselves into a commanding position, we didn't let it all slip away.

I needn't have worried. Real Madrid appeared to be in a state of stupor, utterly stunned by the turnaround and mesmerised by the magical feet of George Best, and that newly negative mindset enabled us to finish in comfortable control.

Over the years I have had plenty of praise for that goal, but I'd like to place on record my indebtedness to the men who did so much to get me through the game, struggling as I was with a gammy knee. My defensive comrades, particularly Nobby and the full-back Tony Dunne, were fantastic. I have never known two men better at covering a big centre-half such as myself, and rarely did they play more superbly than on that unforgettable night at the Bernabeu. Oh, and George Best, he deserved a vote of thanks from this old feller, as well!

Before the final of the 1968 European Cup, the pundits had predicted that a United winger would tear the Portuguese rearguard to shreds, and so one did, but most observers agreed afterwards that the man of the match was not the genius Best – although the Irishman did make a colossal contribution towards the outcome – but the frequently vilified Aston.

John was a pragmatic, down-to-earth young fellow who had not found life to be easy after breaking into the senior side. A titanic worker and unfailingly brave, he was not gifted with extravagant talent and thus, when things went wrong for the team, he was often singled out by terrace morons who were desperate for a scapegoat but loath to pillory such heroes as Best, Law and Charlton. In addition, the undemonstrative Mancunian had to live down the circumstance that his father, also John Aston, had been a top player and something of a crowd favourite in Matt Busby's first great United side in the years immediately following the Second World War. Now John Snr was a coach at Old Trafford and so, in addition to the rest of the venomous claptrap directed his way, the younger Aston had to cope with hysterical and wholly misleading accusations of nepotism. In truth, the family link worked to the detriment of the boy because his father was harder on him than on any of his teammates, realising that not only must he be scrupulously fair, he must also be seen to be so, thus sometimes being stricter with his own flesh and blood than with other members of the squad.

But on that balmy evening at Wembley, when battle-hardened Benfica were contesting

Tense and focused on the night of their footballing lives, John Aston (left), George Best and Bill Foulkes wave to the fans who turned Wembley into Old Trafford South ahead of the 1968 European Cup final.

their fifth European Cup final of the decade while United were lining up for the first in their history, Aston demonstrated his true mettle, proving conclusively that he was the man for a big occasion. After noting that the Portuguese defence had a tendency to play square, he ran them ragged, lacerating the right-back Adolfo, in particular, with his blistering pace, and although none of his steady stream of crosses into the Benfica box resulted in a goal, John Aston played a gigantic part in the ultimate triumph. While he could walk away with a smile of typically modest satisfaction on his face, his exhausted opponents could only limp off in dismay, wondering why all their pre-match talk had been about Best and Charlton, while practically no attention had been paid to the lad who had spent much of the season as an Old Trafford aunt sally.

In the first half of the game at Wembley alone, George was dumped on to the lush turf half a dozen times – usually tripped or smashed, once even hurled – and his patience began to wear thin. Benfica boss Otto Gloria had evidently identified the Irishman as United's principal threat and, for all the Portuguese protestations of innocence, there was

The gesture says it all. After the latest of a series of wild assaults on his person, George Best is making it plain to the offenders, and to Italian referee Concetto Lo Bello – the official who had presided over the Irishman's destruction of Benfica at their own Stadium of Light two seasons earlier – that he thinks his persecutors are bonkers.

clearly a concerted campaign to nullify him by fair means or foul. Cruz was the main hatchet man, but it was Humberto who ended up being booked.

The first 45 minutes of the game were unbearably tense, and while United looked the stronger team it was Benfica who came closest to scoring, when the magnificent Eusebio shot against the woodwork with United goalkeeper Alex Stepney helpless to intervene. The otherwise excellent David Sadler missed United's best chance, and frustration had begun to mount when Best's old digs mate facilitated the breakthrough after 53 minutes, floating a cross from the left touchline which was met by the balding head of the leaping, twisting Charlton. The ball glanced perfectly off his pate to describe a tantalising arc beyond the floundering Jose Henrique, then dropped just inside the far post.

Now there seemed no question that Busby's men would yield the initiative, but on a muggy, fearfully draining evening they tired perceptibly in the last quarter of an hour of the second half. With only nine minutes left, the beanpole Jose Torres outsprung the valiant veteran Foulkes, the Munich survivor in his thirty-seventh year, for the first time in the contest and the ball bounced down for the elegant midfielder Jaime Graca to equalise from a narrow angle.

Suddenly, for a brief but horrifying interlude, United were dangerously vulnerable and when Eusebio slipped free of his warder Nobby Stiles and bore down on Alex Stepney with the ball at his feet, the prospect of demoralising defeat loomed large. However, instead of seeking to place the ball into the net in sensible, economical style, the 'Black Panther' opted for the sensational, hammering it with all his might, and with his slightly less reliable left foot. The shot thudded into the midriff of Stepney, he held on brilliantly and cleared upfield, ignoring in his total concentration the sporting gesture of Eusebio in applauding his remarkable save. In retrospect, that was the turning point of the final. Though soon the referee was blowing his whistle to signal extra time, and every last one of United's 22 legs was aching with fatigue, the blue-shirted Red Devils were now convinced that this was their night.

The first period of added time was only three minutes old when Shay Brennan knocked the ball back to Alex Stepney, who picked it up and launched a long-distance clearance up the field. As the missile dropped from the gathering gloom of the night sky, it was glanced on by Brian Kidd into the path of George Best, whose pace and trickery took him beyond the immediate beefy challenge of Jacinto (above) and rendered the posse of desperately

It is one of the most iconic images of the Irishman's life and it hangs on the walls of countless supporters all over the globe – with 27 minutes to go, the Eagles' dreams of a European Cup final win were dashed.

back-pedalling Portuguese defenders utterly irrelevant. That left the darting Irishman with only the keeper in his way and he wrong-footed Henrique comprehensively with a giddying swerve, then sidefooted the ball between the unattended posts, even as the custodian strove gamely but unavailingly to get back. Later, with characteristic drollery, the affable Brennan claimed an 'assist' for his part in the pivotal goal in the biggest game in Manchester United's history.

Bobby Charlton engulfs George in a bear hug after the Irishman had scampered to congratulate him for scoring his second goal of the game, the one which gave their team a surely unassailable 4–1 lead.

With the ball safely in the back of the net, George Best turned to celebrate with his teammates and the gathered multitude, the vast majority of whom were rooting for United. Although there were still 27 minutes left to play, the mighty Eagles had been well and truly grounded. They were a spent force and their total collapse over the next seven minutes rendered the second period of extra time one of pure exultation for every man, woman and child who marched under the Manchester United banner, or who merely wished them well from the comfort of their armchairs. George Best had delivered majestically, and with superlative timing, when it really mattered most.

Only some 60 seconds after the Irishman's dazzling solo effort, Brian Kidd marked his nineteenth birthday with United's third goal, a clever nodded follow-up after his first header from Sadler's knock-on following a Charlton corner had bounced back off the

Wreathed in smiles the pair turn to share their joy with the rest of the team.

crossbar. Thus the Collyhurst Kidd enjoyed a moment that even Roy of the Rovers' script-writer might have hesitated to pen, and United rolled on inexorably.

Bobby's second with some 21 minutes of the contest remaining rounded off a night of euphoria and supreme fulfilment, and a decade of tragedy, trial and frustration.

◄ One of George's most genuinely heartfelt celebrations took place with David Sadler. The pair of them had started at Old Trafford together as a couple of shy teenagers, and while it might be fair to admit that the Kentishman remained a tad more retiring than the boy from Burren Way as the years sailed by, there always remained between them an unshakeable bond. George, putting the violence of his treatment at the hands, and feet, of the Portuguese defenders to one side now the contest had been won, has swapped shirts with one of his tormentors, but David has opted to retain his blue top.

DAVID SADLER: *George and I had some fabulous footballing times together, and this one topped the lot. It's fair to say that John Aston was our outstanding player on the night, but George was terrific, too, not least by creating space for the rest of us by occupying so many of the Benfica defenders, who were terrified of the damage he could do.*

Matt Busby might be bursting forth with a rendition of one of his favourite songs, Louis Armstrong's 'What A Wonderful World', as he dances a little jig while brandishing a facsimile of the European Cup with a similarly elated George Best. The colourful, voluble, frequently hilarious Paddy Crerand, on the other hand, concentrates on the real thing, which George also manages to clutch.

Nobody should under-estimate the part Crerand played in that Wembley triumph. Alongside Bobby Charlton in United's creative engine-room in centre-field, the flinty, occasionally irascible Glaswegian had never stopped working, despite the stifling heat which enveloped the famous old stadium. During his pomp, the incisiveness of his passing was not bettered anywhere in the English game, and not for nothing did one shrewd observer of the First Division scene declare: 'When Crerand plays well, then United play well.'

Paddy tended to be the life and soul of most parties, too, but ironically, on the night of the victory over Benfica he, like Charlton, missed most of the post-match high jinks because he felt so ill, partly through dehydration brought on by his gargantuan efforts on Wembley's lush acres in the humid heat, and partly through sheer exhaustion, both physical and emotional.

PADDY CRERAND: *I've often thought that if George Best had been born ugly, he would have played until he was 50. He was a great footballer, but he was getting the type of publicity that no player before him had experienced. Footballers had never been front page news before, or certainly not on a regular basis like George. Add the circumstance that he was a good-looking lad to the fact that he was getting a bit of publicity and he was bound to be attractive to women. All the public exposure that followed was bound to cause a problem or two – if only he had looked like the back of a bus!*

But for all that happened he was always fanatical about his football. George did everything that much later we heard of Eric Cantona doing with that glorious squad of young players that included Beckham, Scholes and the rest. He would be out there on the training pitch long after the official session had finished, taking free-kicks, doing shooting drills, just for fun.

In their time together, George gave Sir Matt both unalloyed joy and serial heartache, the Irishman's phenomenal talent as a footballer partly balanced, but certainly never outweighed, at least in historical terms, by the serial problems he caused by his off-the-field misdemeanours.

Fundamentally there was between the two men a tremendous affection that never withered, despite all the frustrations Busby endured on account of his wayward prodigy. Perhaps it's fair to say, though, that they never truly and thoroughly understood each other.

It didn't help that George's rise to prominence coincided with the eruption of youth culture in the 1960s. Suddenly, in a short space of time, he was catapulted from being a waif nursing a dream on the tough streets of Belfast to become a superstar almost on a par with the Beatles. Even that might not have precipitated the fracture which followed but for one unfortunate circumstance, namely that he had nobody to turn to for advice who had experienced similar adulation. Equally, Sir Matt had never witnessed such a phenomenon before and wasn't sure how to address it.

On top of that, at the time George was attaining his global celebrity, Sir Matt was not in the best of health, never having quite recovered from Munich, and he could have done

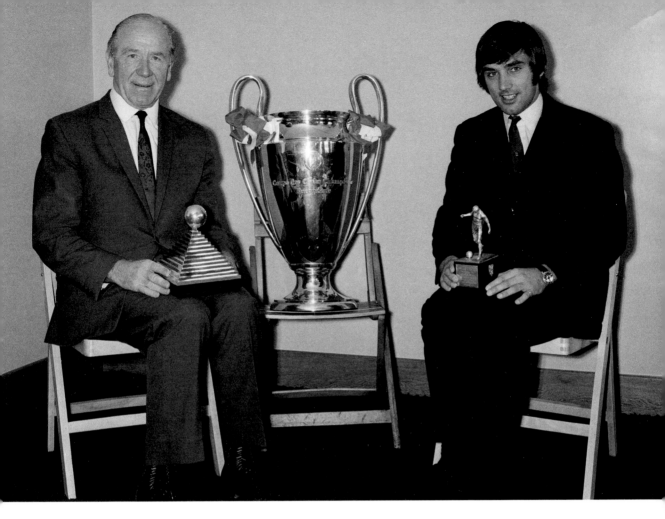

without the thorny conundrum poised by his errant star. Soon after United's Wembley triumph, the manager said: 'Let us hope this is not the end, just the beginning.' Alas, it was not to be.

Here, two men who scaled the loftiest pinnacles together with Manchester United and who also, in their vastly differing ways, plumbed the most profound depths, sit rather stiltedly for the camera, displaying the spoils of their recent endeavours.

Between them, perched artlessly on a folding chair, is the European Cup, the trophy which symbolises ultimate achievement and some sort of closure for Matt Busby, in the wake of his continental trailblazing and the loss of so many of his beloved Babes at Munich ten years earlier. On his knee is the bauble he received as Manager of the Year, while George Best, as neatly besuited as his boss and mentor, clutches the Footballer of the Year statuette.

9

ANXIOUS TIMES
1968/69

9
ANXIOUS TIMES
1968/69

Expectations were high for Manchester United in the summer of 1968, but some debilitating slip-ups were in the immediate offing. Still, it was taken as a given that Best was on an inexorable rise, and it was very rare at this point that he would say 'no' to a cameraman. Here, in central London in July 1968, some eight weeks after shining in the European Cup final victory over Benfica at Wembley, he is hamming it up on a borrowed bicycle, the basis for the picture being that he had just been given a six-month driving ban and therefore would have to resort to two wheels. As if!

The sentence, which also included a £25 fine – a telling reflection on the rate of inflation over the last four decades – was handed down by a Manchester court for his part in an accident at Crumpsall, in the north of the city, in the early hours of a December morning. This time his behaviour on the road appears to be impeccable, as he's stopped close to the kerb at a zebra crossing. In reality, of course, it would have been rash to conclude that he had learnt his lesson.

Fashion note: the shirt and slacks are pretty timeless, but the beige corduroy bomber jacket with cuffs turned back will revive a few memories for fellows of a certain age.

▲ The venue is Old Trafford, George Best is playing for Manchester United and Mike Summerbee is representing City, but it's unlikely that the two friends and sometime business partners are too bothered about the outcome of this particular contest.

The teams donned their spotless flannels to meet at the headquarters of Lancashire County Cricket Club, half a mile along the old Warwick Road from the football ground, in a game to support the benefit year of Ken Higgs, the tireless medium-fast bowler who made his name for the Red Rose before excelling for England.

Is George asking the grinning Mike if he has always been that lucky after edging a boundary past third man, or is he taking him to task for breaching cricket etiquette by sporting dark socks under his whites? Perhaps a more realistic bet is that the sociable duo are debating where to go for their next night out. As to the outcome of the game, United batted first and assembled the paltry total of 79 runs, enabling City to triumph by six wickets, with Francis Lee smiting an unbeaten 36.

At this distance, Mike can't recall the scorecard details, but what remains clear down the years is that, as a footballer, he was one of the finest going, an attacker both talented and fearsomely feisty, and certainly a key component of the City side which overhauled United in the final straight to lift the League championship of 1967/68.

MIKE SUMMERBEE: *The cricket was a lot of fun and there were more people watching us than turned up for an England v West Indies game that I remember at Old Trafford.*

As for my socks, I wasn't seeking attention, it was just that I didn't have a pair of white ones. Probably if George rolled up his trousers you'd find that he wasn't wearing any, never mind the wrong colour.

From the moment he and I met by chance in the Kardomah coffee house in St Anne's Square, Manchester, shortly after I had signed for City in 1965, there was a chemistry between us which deepened quickly into a genuine friendship. Our relationship wasn't about football, we barely mentioned it. Even in the Manchester derby we'd keep out of each other's way on the pitch. Beforehand I'd say something like: 'Don't start taking the mick out of me. If you stick the ball through my legs I'll have to give you a whack! Then we won't be going out tonight.' He'd say: 'Okay, I'll see you tonight then!'

We had a fantastic time together. I was more of an open talker, while George was quiet, but he had the looks. He was a superstar but that didn't make a scrap of difference. I knew he was a genius while I was just a reasonably good player, but that never came into the equation. Friendship is one of the most important things in life, and my relationship with George epitomised that.

As players, Nobby Stiles and George Best were poles apart but they did rejoice in mutual respect and affection. For all the plucky little Mancunian's lurid image as a ravening brute, raw in tooth and claw, who would kick his opponents over the stand, or tear out their throats before wiping his fangs on the corner flag, George understood that Stiles was, in fact, an exceptionally gifted footballer endowed with one of the most subtle attributes any player can possess.

In addition to all the normal accomplishments of any top performer – controlling the ball assuredly, passing it accurately, being proficient when it was in the air, and so on – Nobby was virtually unsurpassed at the key skill of reading the game, anticipating the action while it was still unfolding, thus allowing him to snuff out potential problems before they become critical. That explained why he was almost always in the right place at the right time, whether he was playing in central defence alongside big Bill Foulkes for Manchester United, or in central midfield with the likes of Bobby Charlton, Alan Ball and Martin Peters for England. It would be difficult to deny, though, that he liked a tackle and he would never shrink from any physical challenge, so it was inevitable that sometimes those in direct opposition might pick up a bruise or three. George loved Nobby as a winner but also as an honest competitor, a quality he recognised in others because it was so deeply ingrained in his own sporting outlook.

Spot the rebel: Nobby Stiles and Bobby Charlton flank George Best at Manchester United's Old Trafford photocall ahead of the 1968/69 campaign, and it comes as no surprise that England's two World Cup winners are wearing their shirts tucked tidily into their shorts, while the young Irishman opts for the casual look. The photographer had not assembled the customary glorious trinity of Best, Law and Charlton, but he was snapping a truly fabulous threesome nevertheless.

Away from the game the pair didn't mix much – Nobby's closest pals were Charlton and the Irish-Mancunian full-back Shay Brennan – but when thrown together on away trips they got on famously. George was never one to accentuate his extreme fame, relishing the chance to be just one of the lads, while when Stiles was off duty he belied his ferocious image by his combination of endearing amiability and almost Inspector Clouseau-like clumsiness. Fans of rival clubs and countries might be astounded by the thought, but it's the absolute truth.

NOBBY STILES: *George didn't fear anything. He was no shrinking violet. He would get the ball at his feet and be ready to face all comers. There were some tough players in those days and their managers would tell them to let George know they were there. Was he bothered? Not a bit of it. He was always ready to try something, to beat players in a different way. Sometimes he would even try to score direct from a corner, and occasionally he'd manage it, such was his fantastic control of the football. He could bend the ball amazingly. He was young, but he was natural, a genius.*

◄ Denis Law and George Best indulge in a spot of topless synchronised running during pre-season work with United at The Cliff training ground in Broughton, Manchester. In truth, the two great footballers are not busting a gut here, rather they're showpiecing their finely honed physiques for the camera. As Denis recalled, it took them hours to get the choreography exactly right!

During their playing days, although they were not the closest of friends because of the contrasting lives they led, there was always a certain chemistry between the pair, perhaps born out of each recognising a streak of devilment in the other.

George Best's much-valued bond with Manchester City's Summerbee puzzled some people because they played for the rival local clubs, but the pair couldn't have cared less about that. At the time they were young bachelors with a similar outlook on life, they had a shared sense of humour and enjoyed socialising together. No problem!

For Mike, of course, the freewheeling lifestyle changed forever when he married Tina Schofield at the lovely little church at Mottram-in-Longendale on the edge of the Peak District in October 1968. The two men remained pals, though, and Mike looked no further than George when it came to choosing his best man.

MIKE SUMMERBEE: *Far from George attracting all the attention on our wedding day, he was totally unassuming and did a fantastic job. That didn't surprise me because he was essentially a shy man. George never hogged the limelight, rather the limelight hogged him. Okay, in some of the pictures it seems as though Tina couldn't take her eyes off him but, let's be fair, he was a great-looking fella!*

George had a terrific sense of humour, as he demonstrated at the back door of the church when we arrived – on time, incidentally, which was unusual for him. As we looked out over the moors he said to me: 'You know, you've only got to walk through that door, run down the field, jump over the wall and you'll be free as a bird. They'd never catch you!' I wasn't remotely tempted, as he knew I wouldn't be, but it was nice of him to point out the possibility!

Given his serial frustration in international football, George Best was understandably excited by the prospect of competing in the World Club Championship. On paper it was one of the game's supreme challenges, the holders of the European Cup facing the champions of South America to decide which was the best club team on the planet. But in the event, Manchester United's two-legged clash with Estudiantes de la Plata of Argentina was nothing less than a poisoned chalice. Any notion of scaling one of professional sport's most rarified peaks was made ridiculous over the course of two scabrously violent encounters in which many of the South Americans behaved shamefully. In the second game, at Old Trafford, blazing mad and utterly frustrated by their cynical approach, the Irishman was sent off for the first time in his life, and it was difficult not to view the experience as an entirely negative one.

Even before the first game, Estudiantes had gone to war, labelling Nobby Stiles as

'brutal, badly intentioned and a bad sportsman' in the match programme, and he was tagged 'El Bandido' in the Buenos Aires press. But when the action started at the Jorge Luis Hirschi stadium it was glaringly apparent that it was the hosts who belonged in a rogues' gallery. George Best was repeatedly targeted with scandalous fouls, Bobby Charlton was lucky to escape without a broken leg from one vicious tackle and poor Stiles was punched and butted in the face by Carlos Bilardo, who then threw himself melodramatically to the ground while protesting that he was the innocent party. Finally, to add insult to injury, the feisty little Mancunian was sent off for making a mild gesture of dissatisfaction when he was judged farcically to be offside, thus being banned for the return leg in Manchester.

Matt Busby, not usually a man to complain about either opponents or officials, was as close to being apoplectic as it was possible to imagine him: 'My team behaved magnificently, refusing to rise to the most naked provocation. Holding the ball out there put a player in danger of his life. It was disgraceful.'

In the light of such controversy, it was easy to overlook the fact that Estudiantes won the game 1–0, thanks to a header by Marcos Conigliaro in the twenty-eighth minute, while David Sadler had what looked a perfectly legal goal disallowed for offside.

Still, United felt they had a realistic chance of overturning the deficit at Old Trafford, but from the moment they conceded an early goal to Ramon Veron – the father of Juan Sebastian Veron, who was destined to sign for the Red Devils in 2001 – the Argentinians never looked like losing. Still George Best, attempting to dance past two of his predatory markers (above), refused to give up and looked the most likely of Busby's men to reduce the deficit, but near the end of a contest during which he had been fouled repeatedly, provoked constantly and even spat at, he finally cracked. Caught by a diabolical challenge from Hugo Medina, he swung a right hook and was dismissed, along with the aggressor. Later he declared that the two meetings with Estudiantes had not been games, but swordfights. He accused the Argentinians of kicking lumps out of the English champions, then diving all over the place as if they were victims rather than culprits. 'Some of their tackles fell just short of murder,' he summed up.

Willie Morgan's late goal made it 1–1 on the night, but Estudiantes won 2–1 on aggregate and noisily proclaimed themselves as world champions. To George and his teammates, that was nothing more than a sick joke.

▲ Such was Best's prodigious all-round talent and exceptional athleticism that often he would attempt breathtaking manoeuvres that lesser players would barely even contemplate. Such a moment occurred when he volleyed spectacularly towards the Ipswich goal at Old Trafford in November 1968. Unfortunately for George, the ball flashed marginally wide of the far upright and the visitors went on to achieve a 0–0 draw, a typically disappointing result in a season of frustrating anti-climax.

There were also tame home draws against West Ham, Arsenal, Leeds and Stoke, while Chelsea, Manchester City and Southampton actually breached United's customary citadel, all leaving Old Trafford with two points. It was a trend that had begun towards the end of the previous campaign, and George began to fret that the side was not being renewed by the addition of top-class recruits.

Airborne again, George has hammered the ball beyond the desperate lunge of Liverpool's centre-half, the Scottish colossus Ron Yeats, but for all the effort and concentration apparent in the Irishman's expression, the Merseysiders' goal remained intact in this incident at Old Trafford in December 1968.

Although United won their home encounter with Liverpool shortly before Christmas, thanks to a lone strike by Denis Law, the Red Devils remained well off the title pace and there was an inescapable feeling abroad that Anfield boss Bill Shankly was reseeding his wonderful team of the 1960s a little more briskly than was his old friend and mentor Matt Busby.

As history would show, United were soon to slump into the doldrums from which they would not fully emerge, in terms of challenging meaningfully for the League crown, until the Alex Ferguson revolution gathered momentum in the early 1990s. In stark contrast, Liverpool would hit new heights during the 1970s and '80s, thanks to a succession of managers – Bob Paisley, Joe Fagan and Kenny Dalglish – in whom the famous Boot Room mentality, entailing paying attention to all the countless little details so that the big ones looked after themselves, had been imbued over many years.

To be fair to Busby, he attempted to secure a similar brand of in-house continuity by putting his former Babe, Wilf McGuinness, in charge of the side in April 1969. Sadly that was not to work out – not that the blame could be laid at Wilf's door – and although George didn't explore his growing worries with teammates at the time, he felt that all was far from right at Old Trafford.

The last day of the 1968/69 season was a tense occasion, with the visitors, Leicester City – who had just lost the FA Cup final to Manchester City and were managed by future United boss Frank O'Farrell – needing a win to retain their top-flight status.

The afternoon started so well for Leicester with a goal by David Nish in the first minute, but three minutes later they were 2–1 down thanks to George's explosive 20-yard strike and another hit by Willie Morgan, then Denis Law made it 3–1 before Rodney Fern pulled one back towards the end, too late to avert the drop.

It was an entertaining finale to United's campaign, but it did nothing to diminish the sharp disappointment of coming eleventh in the First Division, wholly inadequate for a club that had kicked off in August anticipating a title challenge and that had finished second, first, fourth, first and second in the five terms in which George had taken part to date. An FA Cup quarter-final defeat by Everton offered no solace, either, though the most crushing reverse came in the most important competition of them all, the European Cup.

The Irishman had believed that, as holders, United had every chance of retaining the trophy, and they did reach the semi-finals, only to lose 2–1 on aggregate to AC Milan. Their exit was controversial. After losing 2–0 at the San Siro, where Milan had ample opportunity to put the outcome beyond doubt, they performed with far more bite and urgency at Old Trafford, and when Bobby Charlton reduced the arrears with a classic scorcher from a narrow angle after 70 minutes following some scintillating Best footwork, a comeback seemed on. Then, seven minutes later, Denis Law got on the end of a subtle little chip from Paddy Crerand and was certain he had poached

◀ It didn't matter how many opponents lined up to close off his avenue to goal and to rob
him of the ball, George Best was ready to take them all on. Here, at Old Trafford on
the last day of season 1968/69, he is confronted by a pair from about-to-be-relegated
Leicester City in a contest United shaded by three goals to two.

the aggregate equaliser, only for the referee to rule out the 'goal', maintaining that the
ball hadn't crossed the line. Denis was sure that it had, declaring his belief with characteristic fervour, and television evidence suggested he was right, as did the testimony
of City-supporting cameraman Eric Graham, who was only a few feet away beside the
net. However, it didn't stand; United were out and although they took the reverse with
commendable dignity, lining up to applaud their conquerors off the field, the players
were understandably bitter.

Thus that season George added no medal to what he believed should be a burgeon-
ing collection and he was not happy. The fact was that when United had triumphed at
Wembley a year earlier he had been only 22 years old and remained massively ambitious.
But he had the unavoidable impression that some people at Old Trafford felt that with
the prize they had chased for so long having been attained, their main job was now done.
In particular, he believed that the manager had won everything he had set out to win,
and as Sir Matt grew older, George surmised that maybe football didn't hold the same
excitement for him any more. The Irishman might have been hurtfully wrong, and if he
had felt that way then certainly he should have brought it out into the open at the time,
but instead he let it eat away at him.

As he told Joe Lovejoy in *Bestie*, his authorised biography (Sidgwick and Jackson, 1998):

I suppose I was spoilt. I'd had success right from day one, and now it was disappearing before my eyes, when I'd really hardly started. We had proved ourselves to be
the best in Europe, and then the next season we were middle of the table and trying
to put it down to the fact that because we were the European champions, everybody
wanted to beat us. The fact is that they shouldn't have been able to. I think quite a
few players thought we had done what we set out to do, and relaxed a bit. I certainly didn't see it that way.

Though he would continue as Manchester United's main attraction for the next few
campaigns, turning in some performances that remain vivid in the memory for their

sheer brilliance over forty years later, his feeling for the club would never be quite the same again.

▶ If George Best and Sir Matt Busby had been peering into a crystal ball – rather than gazing at the Ballon D'Or trophy awarded to the Irishman as European Footballer of the Year for 1968 – both men might have been more than a little disturbed at what they could perceive of the future.

At this point, on the pitch at Old Trafford shortly before George scored one of the two goals that beat Burnley in the penultimate fixture of an admittedly disappointing season, the pair might have been sanguine about their prospects. After all, Best was still only 22 years old and was being feted as the leading light of the continental game, while being hailed universally as one of the top players anywhere around the globe. Busby, meanwhile, was contemplating what he hoped would be a tranquil and fulfilling semi-retirement, having relinquished day-to-day responsibility for the Manchester United team to young Wilf McGuinness, while retaining an overall influence by 'moving upstairs' to become general manager.

Sadly George, who had achieved so much so young, and must have expected plenty more honours to be placed alongside his medals for winning the European Cup and two League titles, would never earn another major prize, while Sir Matt would face years of trauma and disillusionment before his beloved United would return once again to football's high places.

For the moment, though, it was right to reflect with enormous pleasure on the remarkable feat of three Red Devils being voted European Footballer of the Year for the third time in five years. Denis Law was top man in 1964, then in 1966 it was Bobby Charlton. In fact, Bobby's status was underlined even more emphatically, as he was runner-up in both 1967 and '68, first to the elegant Hungarian centre-forward Florian Albert and then to George.

Both off the field and on it, George Best was the footballing pin-up of the ages. In the late '60s, he was the boy who had the lot – the classically handsome dark looks; the twinkling blue eyes; the slim, resilient physique; an engaging nature unscarred by any apparent baseness; and, of course, that natural, unique, untouchable talent.

As time went on the constant attention of photographers, became painful to him, but after putting aside his initial shyness, he came to enjoy being the focus of the flashing lights. He was willing to cultivate publicity as a tool to promote his business interests and although there were times when he must have felt like an exhibit in a zoo, he was willing to play that particular game, not appreciating exactly where it might lead.

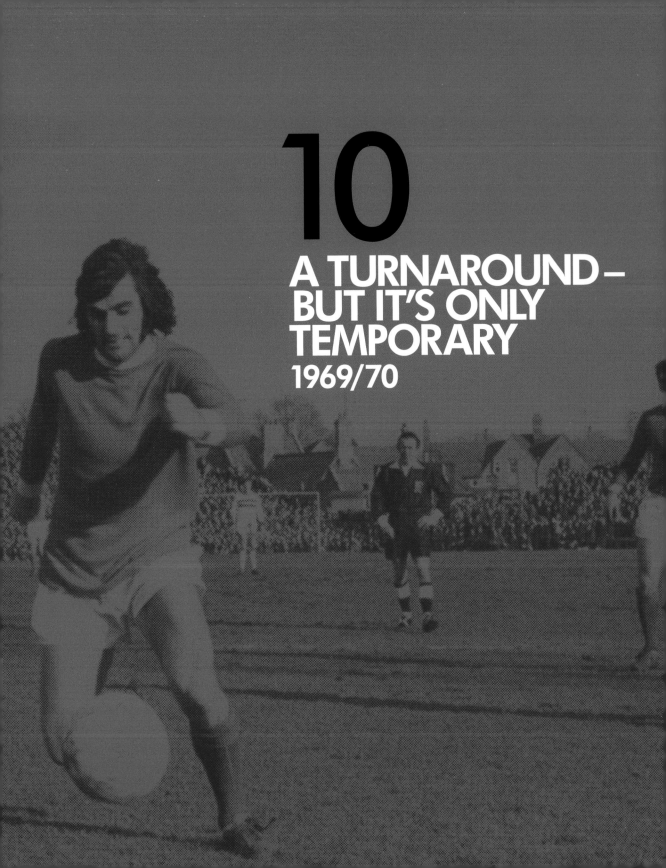

10

A TURNAROUND – BUT IT'S ONLY TEMPORARY

1969/70

10
A TURNAROUND – BUT IT'S ONLY TEMPORARY
1969/70

The new campaign opened in August with a match against newly promoted Crystal Palace at Selhurst Park and marked a milestone for Manchester United, as the first competitive game for nearly a quarter of a century for which Matt Busby wasn't in charge of the team, the task going instead to new chief coach Wilf McGuinness.

The 2–2 draw with Palace didn't represent a disastrous start in itself, but it was followed by three defeats – for one of which, at Everton, Wilf did the hitherto unthinkable by dropping Bobby Charlton and Denis Law. Then came two more draws and with them the inevitable headlines about a club in crisis.

The trouble was that in comparison to Busby, who exuded gravitas, on a scale equalled by no other figure in the game, the eager and voluble Wilf appeared almost schoolboyish. Certainly George thought 31-year-old McGuinness was too young for such a colossal responsibility, and that he would have been better off proving himself elsewhere before taking United's reins, but the Irishman liked the effervescent Mancunian personally and was willing to give him a chance.

However, George perceived that some of the older players were less accommodating towards their new leader and the team spirit was suffering in consequence, a situation which depressed and worried him profoundly. He recognised, too, that McGuinness had inherited serious playing problems, with many of the top men beginning to show signs of age while the kids who had risen through the ranks were not of the same calibre as the previous generation of Busby Babes.

Against this background it's remarkable that Best was so instrumental in bringing

◄ Bobby Charlton and George Best, two of the most dazzling performers ever to grace the game, line up to face a Crystal Palace free-kick.

about a temporary turnaround in United's fortunes that autumn, scoring 11 goals in a ten-game sequence in which they lost only one League game and rose from near the foot of the table to eighth place by early November.

Still, though, George was plagued by doubts about the team's future, and as results fell away alarmingly during the winter he grew increasingly disillusioned at United's drop in standard. Accordingly, though manifestly their most influential performer, he found it more and more difficult to motivate himself. He was no longer so assiduous about turning up for training on time, knowing perfectly well that he would be better than virtually all the rest anyway. It was not a healthy trend.

◄ George Best and Eric McMordie had come a long way from the pair of fearful waifs who had crossed the Irish Sea in the summer of 1961. In September 1969, Eric was part of the Middlesbrough side about to face United in a League Cup tie which the hosts would shade 1–0, courtesy of a goal by another close pal of Best, David Sadler. On McMordie's first visit a decade earlier the lads were virtual lookalikes – small, skinny, short-haired and oozing anxiety on their first substantial trip away from home. Eight years on George, with his sculpted locks, was comfortably the trendier of the two, and by far the most successful in terms of achievement, although Eric hadn't done badly by any means, managing to forge a worthy career in the professional game after initially believing that his Old Trafford disappearing act had scuppered his hopes.

After working as a plasterer while playing for the Belfast part-timers Dundela FC, he was spotted and recruited by Middlesbrough, signing early in the 1964/65 campaign in which George helped United to land the League title. McMordie went on to play some 250 games for the Teessiders, also serving Sheffield Wednesday on loan, York City and Hartlepool before leaving the Football League in 1978. At his peak he had been a neat, clever inside-forward and he collected 21 caps for Northern Ireland, most of them alongside George.

PAT JENNINGS: *Only once do I recall getting the better of George in a one-on-one situation. It was in an FA Cup replay at White Hart Lane in January 1968 which we went on to win. He was through on goal, having gone past two or three of our defenders, and I managed to get down to his feet and nick the ball. It wasn't often that you could do that because his brain was like lightning and he did things a yard quicker than anybody else.*

See you later, pal! George Best gives the swerve to his close chum Pat Jennings during Manchester United's 3–1 victory over Tottenham Hotspur at Old Trafford in November 1969. Best and Jennings made their Northern Ireland debuts in the same game but, despite their friendship and their brilliance at their respective crafts, the two men were utterly different in outlook. Pat was reliable, as rock-steady as a fellow could be, and George . . . wasn't.

George Best, looking daggers, is being ushered away to the dressing room by trainer Jack Crompton (back to the camera) and team boss Wilf McGuinness (centre) after a petty contretemps with referee Jack Taylor (right) at the end of United's 2–1 defeat by Manchester City in the first leg of a League Cup semi-final clash at Maine Road in December 1969.

At the turn of the decade, George Best was becoming embroiled in unsavoury on-pitch incidents with worrying frequency, as his frustration with his footballing lot grew ever more oppressive. United's 2–1 defeat by City in the first leg of a League Cup semi-final clash at Maine Road in December 1969 had been a stormy encounter, replete with stiff physical challenges, and for most of the evening a draw had seemed a result both fair and likely. The hosts had gone in front through an early strike by Colin Bell, then Best, who was on top form, started the move which led to Bobby Charlton equalising just after the hour.

The smouldering tension to be expected in any derby burst into flame shortly after that when George, taking issue with the award of a free-kick to City, was booked for booting the ball away in a state of pique. It was an incident that irritated the

Irishman intensely and his mood darkened further when City got what proved to be the winner through a controversial Francis Lee penalty only two minutes from the end. To put it bluntly, the United camp was convinced that the England international had dived theatrically, while Lee maintained stoutly that he had been fouled. Even after that George thought he had saved the day with a header, only to see the ball hacked off the line, and he was still smarting with perceived injustice when he became involved in a heated exchange with referee Jack Taylor as they left the field. His feelings got the better of him and he knocked the ball out of the Wolverhampton butcher's hands, an act which that stern official had no intention of taking lightly.

Duly he included Best's intervention, which was admittedly childish but certainly not malicious, in his match report. The incident was replayed endlessly on television, and it was decided to make an example of him. Thus he became one of the first footballers to be charged with bringing the game into disrepute and he was banned for four weeks and fined £100, a draconian punishment at a time when his disciplinary record was still better than most.

Later George genuinely regretted his transgression, but he felt keenly that he had brought the game into disrepute far less than defenders who spent whole matches kicking him. As he put it graphically: 'There are people out there who break other players' legs, and they don't get punished so severely.'

There was more turmoil in the second leg at Old Trafford, which finished 2–2, enough to see City through to Wembley on a 4–3 aggregate. Ian Bowyer scored first for the visitors, putting them in an exceedingly strong position, but then they were pegged back by a fulminating 20-yarder from United's rookie defender Paul Edwards. McGuinness's men seized the upper hand in the second half and Best set up an overall equaliser when he climaxed a typically magical sortie down the right flank with a rasping shot. City custodian Joe Corrigan couldn't grasp hold of the ball and Denis Law stabbed in the rebound. Now United looked the likely winners, but they bowed out through a moment's understandable misjudgement by their keeper Alex Stepney. City were awarded an indirect free-kick on the edge of United's box, and Lee slammed the ball goalwards with characteristic brio. Had Stepney allowed the missile to pass him by, all would have been serene. But in the heat of the moment he parried Lee's effort, and the ball fell to Mike Summerbee and he poked it into the net. It was a grim moment for United in general, but particularly so for poor McGuinness, whose long-term employment prospects were severely diminished by the cruel defeat.

As the new decade dawned, stories about George Best's boozing became common currency in the popular press. It appears that he first started drinking to overcome his natural shyness, particularly with girls, then later the alcohol provided an escape valve from what he saw as the deteriorating situation at Manchester United. No doubt he attracted his share of hangers-on, but also he had a close coterie of genuine friends. It's profoundly sad that they were unable to help him to overcome the darkness that enveloped him.

Certainly Sir Matt was desperate to save George from himself, even offering him a chance to join the Busby household at one point, but the veteran manager always struggled to come to terms with the chaotic 'scene' which swirled around his ceaselessly in-demand superstar. As he wrote in *Soccer at the Top* (Weidenfeld & Nicolson, 1973):

Wherever he went, swarms of people enveloped him, friends, hangers-on, small boys, dear old ladies and an inevitable gaggle of girls, who seemed to be attracted like moths to a light . . . I would have had to be blind and deaf not to be aware about some of the capers he got up to, or was rumoured to get up to, that were not within a footballer's accepted curriculum. I would have him up in my office and play the very devil with him.

George spoke of this himself, grinning disarmingly as he admitted: 'I was in his office more than he was. I had my own chair!'

Sir Matt again:

George Best and I did not disagree. He knew perfectly well that he was letting me down every time he let himself down and let the club down. And he always apologised. We fined him. We suspended him. What more could we do? We couldn't shoot him. We might have felt like smacking his bottom, as a man might smack his own son's bottom. But this is not allowed in a player's contract . . . I know that George Best underneath is a good, generous, kindly lad . . . he ran away from problems instead of facing them. But I set great store by patience. We had to hope that he would be cured, this the greatest entertainer, the world's most gifted player who, man and boy, filled football grounds wherever he played, and made people gasp and laugh by his sheer audacity.

Best offered the last great challenge in Busby's career, one in which he had overcome mountainous odds to bounce back from unspeakable agony, both physical and mental, to lead his beloved Manchester United to unprecedented glory. That he failed to guide his flawed genius towards lasting professional fulfilment and, perhaps, personal salvation was both understandable and unbearably poignant.

▶ It's fair to say that when two of the greatest British footballers of all time, Tom Finney and George Best, found themselves together at a function in December 1969, they hailed from opposite ends of the fashion spectrum, but when it came to love of the game they were two peas from the same pod. Though both men were sublimely gifted, and both started as wingers but were capable of filling any attacking role, also both were engagingly modest, so there was no talking directly about their immense achievements, rather some light-hearted banter about George's beard and how there was very little facial hair on display in the older man's day.

For those too young to recall Tom in his imperious prime, suffice it to say that no less canny a judge than Bill Shankly, the architect of the modern Liverpool, earmarked the 'Preston Plumber' as the finest player he had ever encountered during a lifetime in football. Finney collected 76 England caps; served the Deepdale club, his sole employer, faithfully between 1940 and 1960, and exuded a wholesome Corinthian ethos that was very much of the age. It's easy enough to reflect that if only George had been more like Tom as a person, then his career would have lasted longer and glittered even more incandescently, but there is no mileage in that. Better by far to offer up thanks to the footballing deities who sent two such magnificent talents to thrill the sporting world.

Composed and determined – just how determined would become vividly apparent during the ensuing hour-and-three-quarters – George Best faces the camera ahead of Manchester United's FA Cup fifth-round tie at Northampton in February 1970.

February 1970 bore witness to a piece of sporting carnage on the grandest scale. Manchester United faced Northampton in an FA Cup fifth round tie, and George Best was in a resolute frame of mind. The Cobblers were unlucky in that the degree of George's relish for the contest was massaged mightily by the fact that it was his first match back in action after his month's suspension for his spat with referee Jack Taylor after the first leg of United's League Cup semi-final meeting with Manchester City. It was a punishment he considered to be hugely excessive and he wouldn't have been human if, on his next appearance for the Red Devils, he had not been motivated to perform at his very peak, perhaps a fraction more than usual.

Fascinatingly, despite his acknowledged pre-eminence in the British game, he felt United had been playing reasonably well in his enforced absence and he experienced a soupçon of insecurity as he approached the Northampton tie. That feeling was heightened, perhaps, by poison pen mail telling him the team would be better off without him, a preposterous notion to anyone who knew the first thing about football, yet nevertheless it carried a certain resonance to George as he prepared for the match. An indication of his state of mind is that during his suspension he trained so hard that on one occasion he collapsed through sheer exhaustion and had to take the next day off.

In the words of David Meek, then of the *Manchester Evening News* and still the doyen of writers on the club's affairs, he was a restless genius hungry for football action. Now he sated that appetite to the full.

Maybe in the long term some Cobblers fans quite relished, in an ironic kind of way, the notoriety of having George Best score six goals against them on one unforgettable winter's afternoon. But no set of professional footballers could ever actually enjoy being given the sort of runaround performed on them by the brilliant Irishman during that 8–2 drubbing.

Northampton's serial tormentor darts between Frank Rankmore (left) and Frank Large to create further mayhem in the early-afternoon sunshine, February 1970.

Fourth Division Northampton had done extremely well to reach the last 16 of the FA Cup, and certainly they had worked hard to earn this plum tie, taking eight games to dispose of Weymouth, Exeter City, Brentwood and Tranmere Rovers. But now they faced Best at his most irresistible and they had no conceivable answer.

The Cobblers' goalkeeper that day was Kim Book, brother of Manchester City skipper Tony Book, and after his ordeal the shell-shocked custodian summed up graphically: 'We hadn't an earthly with Best in that form. Not even the Berlin Wall could have stopped him. The man was brilliant, fantastic, fabulous. I don't think any of us knew where to look for him. We never knew where he was. The spaces he found were amazing and he always seemed to be in the right spot at the right moment. It was uncanny. Every time the ball went to him I thought to myself: "Hell, here comes another!"'

▲ In the words of Long John Baldry – 'Let the heartaches begin . . .' For Northampton, that is, as George Best leaps above his would-be marker to nod United into a 1–0 lead in the twentieth minute. Soon afterwards he added a second to make it 2–0 at the interval, but it was in the second period that he really hit his twisting, turning, jinking stride. Rarely has an English ground played host to such a ravishing exhibition of dribbling and finishing by the same player. Best simply bamboozled the Northampton rearguard repeatedly as he scored four more goals and still found time to create the second of

Brian Kidd's brace. That night, as he basked in the glory of his spectacular display, he reflected on the tantalising possibility of realising his oldest dream, the one that came to him repeatedly as he chased a ball around the Belfast backstreets, the one of playing in the FA Cup final at Wembley. Alas, it was not to be, not this season, not ever.

WILF McGUINNESS: *The one game from my reign as manager of Manchester United that will always be remembered is our 8–2 FA Cup victory at Northampton, because that was the day on which George scored a double hat-trick. I shall never forget him leaning on a post, after knocking in his sixth of the afternoon, and looking up as if to say: 'Is that enough?' The truth was that when he played like that, nobody could ever get enough of George Best.*

The spring of 1970 brought a grimly combative trilogy of FA Cup semi-final confrontations with Don Revie's formidable Leeds United, a team packed with hugely talented individuals who, to put it mildly, also knew how to look after themselves.

The first game, at Sheffield Wednesday's atmospheric arena, finished 0–0. So did the replay at Villa Park, with Leeds prevailing 1–0 in the third encounter at Burnden Park, thus thwarting George's long-held ambition to grace Wembley in what was still, at that time, the gala showpiece of the domestic game.

When Leeds arrived in Birmingham for the first replay, they were greeted with the news that George had been discovered by Manchester United boss Wilf McGuinness in a girl's bedroom at their team hotel, only a few hours before the match. Though realising that such disruptive behaviour by their most dangerous opponent could only work in Leeds' favour, Johnny Giles was outraged by what he perceived as total disrespect for his former club and for the game itself. As a result he took Best to task during the contest, informing him that as a professional footballer he was an utter disgrace, and kicking him

George Best flat out in the Hillsborough mud after yet another collision with his frequent nemesis, the Leeds right-back Paul Reaney.

under the guise of making a fair challenge – it should be noted here that Giles, a magnificently inventive play-maker and one of the sharpest thinkers the modern game has known, was no stranger to subtly exacting physical retribution when he deemed it necessary.

Whether or not it was as a consequence of George's earlier extra-curricular activities, which rendered the long-suffering and usually amiable McGuinness virtually apoplectic, he was nowhere near the top of his form at Villa Park, his growing chagrin completed by a gross and utterly uncharacteristic error which probably cost his team their place in the FA Cup final. Late in the second half George, for once, wriggled clear of Reaney's close attention and bore down unattended on the Leeds goal. He was a racing certainty to stroke a shot past crouching custodian Gary Sprake to win the match, but instead he trod on the ball and lay face down in the cloying Villa Park quagmire, probably wishing that the pitch could have opened and swallowed him up. Cue derision from the travelling Yorkshire hordes and despair for the Manchester fans, who could be forgiven for feeling that, over the course of the two pulsating encounters, their side deserved marginally to prevail.

However, when they lost the second replay at Bolton through an early strike by Billy Bremner, Manchester United were condemned to a second successive trophyless campaign and the future began to look increasingly ominous for Wilf McGuinness.

WILF McGUINNESS: *As a young manager doing my best to do the virtually impossible, to follow in the footsteps of Sir Matt Busby, I inherited George Best. As a player he was an absolute joy, and I revelled in his beautiful skill. He could do anything, to me he was the eighth wonder of the world, but soon he was causing me difficulties that even Sir Matt hadn't been able to deal with. My job was training, coaching and selection, while Matt retained responsibility for wages, transfers and discipline. In the circumstances we were juggling George between us, and you might say there were a couple of instances when I had to nod a problem on to Matt.*

For instance, there was the infamous occasion when I found him in a hotel bedroom with a girl on the day of our FA Cup semi-final with Leeds at Villa Park. I must emphasise that when I walked through the door the pair of them were sat on the bed, fully clothed and having a chat, but it was a clear breach of discipline which Matt duly dealt with. Because of this incident, people got the misleading impression that he was in the habit of bedding girls on match days on a regular basis, but this was utter hogwash. It's hardly a shocking revelation to say that George was pursued constantly by beautiful

For once George Best has stolen a yard from his remorseless minder Paul Reaney (second left) but wildly muffs his snapshot at the Leeds goal during the two Uniteds' initial FA Cup semi-final deadlock at Hillsborough. Looking on but powerless to intervene are Leeds' Peter Lorimer (left) and Jack Charlton.

young ladies, and I don't think I'm going to stun anyone by adding that he was an exceedingly willing target. But almost always, or so I liked to believe, his football and his love life were kept well apart. It's impossible to say whether George's dalliance with the girl in the hotel had any bearing on the fact that he under-performed in the game at Villa Park. Had he put away that chance in the second half – and I would have bet my house on him scoring with only Sprake to beat – then I believe we would have made it to the FA Cup final and my career path might have been radically altered. But I was never one to wring my hands about what might have been. The fact was that Paul Reaney, a terrific player, did a very fine marking job on George, as he usually did. Afterwards somebody joked that the girl in the hotel was a Leeds United plant. One wag even wondered whether she might have been Paul Reaney in drag, but I never bought into that particular conspiracy theory. I think George might have noticed!

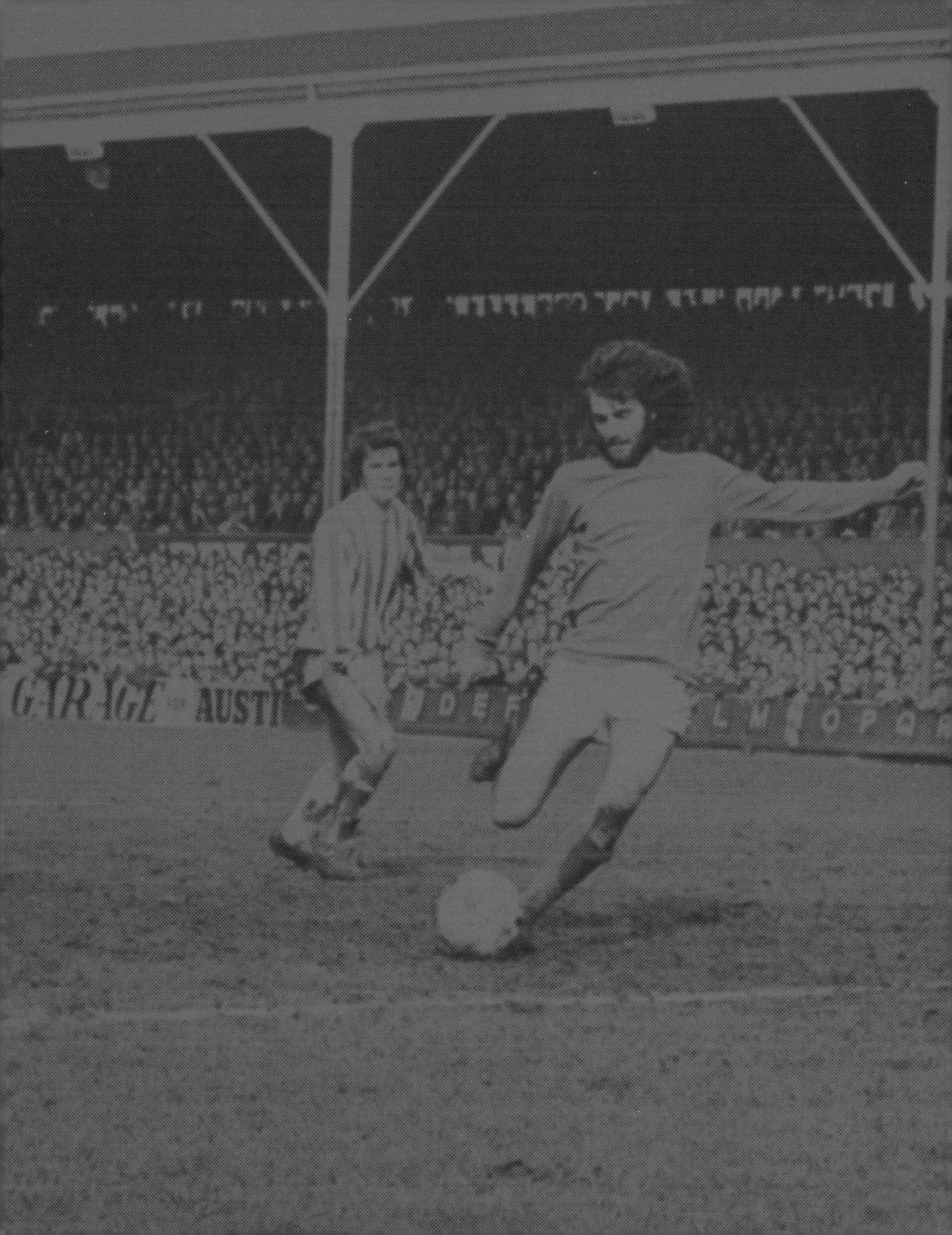

GARAGE
AUSTI
DEF
LMOPQR

11
ON THE SLIPPERY SLOPE
1970/71

11
ON THE
SLIPPERY SLOPE
1970/71

Like pretty well any football men on the threshold of a new season, Wilf McGuinness and George Best were brimming with good cheer during a training session at The Cliff one sunny day in the summer of 1970 (opposite). On the face of it, both men had every reason for optimism. After serving a year as chief coach, 32-year-old McGuinness had just been promoted to the rank of Manchester United's team manager, while Best, still only 24, ought to have been on the verge of his prime. Alas, all too soon the pair of them would be engulfed in trauma.

Wilf's elevation to such lofty status dumbfounded many observers, who cited his lack of experience and the awkwardness he might feel at dealing with players the same age or older than himself and who were his friends, although close examination of his record offers a slightly different perspective. After his United and England playing career was halted cruelly by injury in his early twenties, Wilf spent nearly a decade on the club's coaching team. He had guided England's youth side to the European Junior Cup in 1964 and had been part of Sir Alf Ramsey's coaching staff which prepared the full England squad ahead of its ultimate glory, the lifting of the World Cup in 1966.

Looking back at the previous campaign, his first in nominal charge of United – although with Sir Matt Busby as an ever-present mentor – he could be reasonably content. Though there was no major silverware in the trophy cabinet – Wilf jokes that he did preside over the Reds' triumph in the *Daily Express* Five-a-side indoor championship – he could point to several compelling positives. He had led United to an eighth-place finish in the First Division, three better than had been attained in Sir Matt's farewell term, and they had reached the semi-finals of both domestic cups, losing both by a single goal.

True, it was a matter for concern that the United board had failed to back him in his quest for new signings. He had wanted Ipswich Town full-back Mick Mills, Sunderland central defender Colin Todd and the Luton Town goal machine Malcolm Macdonald, all

of whom were precociously promising youngsters who would go on to hugely successful careers. In retrospect, that lack of support and apparent absence of faith in the judgement of the man they had selected to take the team forward, begs some tantalising questions. Specifically, what difference would the acquisition of three such richly talented youngsters have made to the destinies of United in general and both McGuinness and Best in particular? George was Wilf's key player and anxiety about the declining quality of the squad seemed to be a major contributory factor to the Irishman's inexorable journey off the rails. With a more settled mind about the club's future, might he have knuckled down and progressed into what would surely have been the golden pomp of late twenties and early thirties, instead of sliding towards footballing oblivion?

It's impossible to say, but what is certain is that 1970/71 panned out disastrously for all concerned. United reached another League Cup semi-final, only to lose calamitously to Third Division Aston Villa, while they struggled demoralisingly near the bottom of the First Division table as yuletide approached.

A cuddle for Annie Best from the eldest of her six children at her and husband Dickie's silver wedding celebration at home in Belfast in the summer of 1970. George doted on his mother and was inconsolable when she died an alcoholic in October 1978, feeling a sense of guilt that he had not spent more time with her during her decline.

When George didn't turn up for training on Christmas morning, Wilf wanted to drop him for the Boxing Day trip to meet Derby County on the basis that it was unfair for everybody else to make the effort while the star man couldn't be bothered. He was talked out of that drastic action by Busby, Best scored and performed brightly in a 4–4 draw, but by then the manager's fate was sealed. The next morning Wilf was called into Busby's office at The Cliff and told that he was sacked.

Sir Matt, the man rightly revered as the founder of the modern Manchester United, was quick to lift morale, which had been sagging badly, and the side climbed from the lower reaches of the First Division table at the turn of the year to eighth place at season's end. It was only ever going to be a temporary solution, though. Dramatic change, and a painfully lengthy period of transition which George Best would not survive as a United man, was on the way.

WILF McGUINNESS: *What was George Best like as a person? He was sharp, witty, funny, intelligent, great fun to be with. He could crack a joke and take the mickey with the best of them. There wasn't an ounce of conceit in him and not once did I see him become aggressive, or even get into a serious argument. I will never call George, and I think people who do so are wrong. His weakness was that he couldn't say 'no'. Fundamentally he was such a lovely lad that he didn't want to let anyone down face to face, even if he didn't want to do what was being asked of him. As a result he ended up either doing too much or not turning up at all and letting you down anyway. Overall, having been close to him as a manager and later, on the after-dinner speaking circuit, even closer as a friend, I can only say that I'm proud to have known him. Before the alcohol took hold of George, you couldn't meet a more charming fellow, and even later, he was a beautiful person if he hadn't had a drink. If he had been on the bottle? Then even he didn't know what sort of person he was . . .*

▶ Even geniuses have to practise, and neither Denis Law nor George Best could be accused of shirking on the training ground in the run-up to the 1970/71 campaign. George had his problems and Denis was being written off in some quarters, but although the Scot had struggled with injuries in recent times, and would never again be quite the irrepressible sniper of earlier years, he had only just turned 30 and still had plenty to give. Indeed, still ahead of him were nearly a century of appearances for Manchester United, a one-season return to Manchester City and a swansong for his country in the 1974 World Cup finals.

Law will always occupy a special place in the hearts of those who saw him in his prime. While George was hallowed for his wizardry and Bobby Charlton revered for his grace and his glory, Denis was loved, not only for the splendour of his play, but for an outlaw streak, an irresistible dash of devilry which set him apart. As Cliff Butler, United's statistician and a man who knows more about the club than anyone else alive, was moved to remark: 'You might say George was for the girls, Bobby was for the dads and Denis was for the lads!'

That affection for 'The Lawman', which rolled down so thunderously from the Old Trafford terraces and stands for more than a decade, was shared by George Best, who once put it thus: 'I love the man. He's one of the greatest players I've ever seen and you just can't be miserable in his company.'

▲ While the Red Devils' First Division form in the autumn of 1970 was largely deplorable, the League Cup did offer some light relief, most memorably in the fourth-round clash with Chelsea at Old Trafford. Here George Best is about to apply the final flourish to a sequence of action which, for countless legions of his admirers around the world, sums up his greatness as a footballer more vividly and more comprehensively than any other. Bobby Charlton had put United in front and John Hollins had equalised before the interval, and now both teams were pushing for a winner. With about 15 minutes remaining, a Chelsea attack had broken down and John Aston, carrying the ball out of defence in United's half, spotted George ahead of him, darting unmarked through the centre of the pitch.

Faithful local boy Aston, the hero of the Red Devils' European Cup triumph of 1968 but not always a favourite with the club's more feckless fans, delivered a perfectly weighted, slightly curving pass into the path of the Irishman's run. He latched on to it like a ravenous hound in pursuit of a hare and as stranded blue-shirted defenders attempted to close in on him from several directions, he bore down on the Londoners' goalkeeper, the excellent Peter Bonetti, who advanced uneasily from his line to meet the threat.

As the sprinting Best neared the edge of the box, he was hit from his right side by the hurtling figure of Ron Harris, the famously combative Chelsea defender who, doubtless peeved at being caught out of position, was desperate to rectify the situation. Chopper Ron's near-horizontal lunge was enough to demolish a stone statue, and for a split-second George's legs buckled.

But, as perfectly balanced and whippily resilient as ever, he somehow retained both his footing and his mental equilibrium as he left Harris prone in the mud and out of the equation. Two strides later, having reached the penalty spot, he was confronted by Bonetti with centre-half Marvin Hinton also poised to pounce. George feinted to dribble left of the hapless custodian, then shimmied and went right, thus opening up the net, into which he deposited the ball from six yards, leaving Hinton and right-back Paddy Mulligan to follow it, ruefully and hopelessly, over the line.

Best, as if acknowledging that he had done something special even by his own exalted standards, sank to his knees, raised his arms as if in thanks to the gods which had bestowed on him his unique gifts, then lowered his head to kiss the turf.

A number of factors beyond its pure brilliance and the fact that it secured a 2–1 win for United contributed to the legendary status of this goal. Somehow the floodlights cutting through the mist which swirled around the Theatre of Dreams that night accentuated the drama, but there was also George's utter defiance in the face of Harris's horrible hack. It was as if he was declaring that the Chelsea hard-man could kick him and try to haul him down, but he was indestructible and he was going to score, no matter what.

It was a classic, treasured moment, perhaps all the more valuable because it offered rare and temporary solace in a chronically disappointing season for United. At that point in late October they had won only four of their 14 League games and George was becoming ever more tricky to handle.

Still, after beating Chelsea, the League Cup appeared to be there for the winning, and duly they disposed of Crystal Palace 4–2 in the quarter-finals. The omens seemed even better when they drew Third Division Aston Villa in the last four but then, horror of horrors, they succumbed 3–2 on aggregate over two legs, the humiliating exit occurring at Old Trafford on the night before Christmas Eve. Suddenly, as the club nosedived into a relegation scrap and full-scale crisis gripped Old Trafford, George's glorious sequence of action of two months earlier might have been in another lifetime.

WILF McGUINNESS: *This goal represented one of the most memorable moments of my time in charge of Manchester United, and probably of George Best's entire career. Unquenchable spirit and sheer genius rolled into one – pure magic!*

◄ George Best's antics in the lead-up to Manchester United's visit to White Hart Lane in December 1970 were causing a severe headache for United boss Wilf McGuinness. George had missed the team's train to London, appearing on the platform just as it was pulling out of the station. It was an offence that merited suspension, but the struggling Reds could ill afford to be without their top man, so he was allowed to play and duly starred in a 2–2 draw, making one goal for Denis Law and scoring the other – his hundredth in the League – after sweetly controlling an awkward delivery from John Fitzpatrick on his chest as he burst through the north Londoners' square back line.

Steve Perryman, who played more games for Spurs than anyone else in their history and who had the unfortunate task that day of tracking the Irishman, offered a stark contrast to Best in that he was a supreme professional who would never dream of letting down his club or his teammates. Without being in George's class when it came to raw talent – but then, who was? – he was a footballer of enviable all-round ability, equally at home in defence or midfield, and a fellow whose strength of character shone through in everything he did.

STEVE PERRYMAN: *The key point here is that my eyes are glued to the football rather than to the swaying figure of George Best. As I progressed in my career, I started to re-alise the importance of being patient before making my challenges. Experience brought home to me that if I committed myself rashly then it wasn't a case of the opponent beating me, it was more a case of me beating myself.*

Of course, it's one thing to say that, quite another to put it into operation against a player of George's calibre. With him there was every chance that, no matter what move I made, he would be that vital little touch ahead of me. I knew that if I dived in early, then he'd be gone. Any pace or hurry that I brought to the situation, he would use against me. Put simply, it was my job to try and deal with him – I emphasise the word try! – while making an attempt to block his path or nick the ball.

It was always dinned into me never to react to a feint, rather to react to what was happening to the ball instead of what a player was doing with his body. Where George was concerned that was easier said than done because he would twist and turn every way imaginable, doing his utmost to send out the wrong signals.

Was I doing a one-on-one marking job here? No way. Our manager Bill Nicholson would never have sanctioned that. It was up to the man who was closest to the ball to get tight and make it difficult for the attacker. Of course, it wasn't always possible . . .

A serious word in your ear, son . . . Sir Matt Busby is not amused and with excellent reason.

When George Best was summoned to London in January 1971 to explain to the Football Association why he had picked up three cautions in the space of 12 months – by modern standards that seems a piffling charge-sheet, indeed! – he performed one of the disappearing tricks for which he was to become renowned. He should have been on the train south with Sir Matt – in charge again after the McGuinness dismissal – at 8.30 that morning to arrive for a 12.30 session at Lancaster Gate, but he was hung over from the excesses of the night before, and missed that one and several more, eventually leaving Manchester Piccadilly at 11.30 with no chance of making his appointment.

That left the United boss in an excruciatingly embarrassing position, but such was his standing with the game's authorities that he managed to persuade them to delay the hearing by 90 minutes until the errant Irishman arrived. When he did so, understandably, Sir Matt was waiting to dispense a few home truths and while exactly what passed between the two men remained private, it's a fair bet that the venerable Scot's words were of the sharp variety. For all his avuncular air, Busby was renowned for wielding an iron fist in a velvet glove, although it's a fact that he allowed his most talented player more latitude than most.

Probably the FA grandees were swayed more by Sir Matt's natural air of authority and mellifluous tones than by any excuses advanced by George, but whatever the truth, he got away with a six-week suspended sentence. However, any hope that he had learned his lesson lasted a mere five days. Once again he missed training and wasn't on the London train for the Chelsea match that Saturday. This time Busby lost patience and sent for John Aston as a replacement. Belatedly Best flew to the capital and arrived at the team hotel in Russell Square to be confronted by a phalanx of pressmen and a crowd of fans, mostly screaming girls. Wanting none of that, he told his taxi-driver to take him to the home of a friend, the Irish actress Sinead Cusack, who lived in a flat in Islington. Alas, he was followed and then besieged, poor Sinead eventually emerging to say that George wanted to be left alone.

When he was still missing on the Monday morning Busby suspended him for two weeks, though he met the manager on the Tuesday and made peace. Sir Matt's take was that George had an unspecified private problem, which had been resolved amicably and now the two were going to start again with a clean slate. For his part, George announced: 'I want to stay with Manchester United until I finish my football. I am going to try as hard as I can to get back to my best.'

At the time his teammate Paddy Crerand told a television reporter: 'If he keeps on going on the way he is, he won't last much longer than another two or three years . . . football is a short life. It needs a strong mind and he's got to buckle down to it. Maybe George gets his head turned a little bit. He is not as fit as he should be or could be. He's got this terrific talent and it's going to waste, that's the terrible shame about it.'

Best himself, still upset by what he saw as a lack of footballing progress at Old Trafford over the past two and a half seasons, appeared to remain a tormented soul, saying: 'I've always been half-hated, half-loved by fans and I don't think it will change either way. Everyone makes mistakes – mine just seem to get more publicity than other people's.'

In one thing, at least at that time, he was wrong. As far as the overwhelming majority of football fans was concerned, he was always loved.

DAVID SADLER: *Although Matt and George got on well on a personal level, I don't believe the Boss knew quite how to handle him. George presented problems which were different to anything Matt had encountered before. He knew nothing about the world of nightclubs, discos and fashion boutiques, he was completely outside the new pop culture which George embraced. Meanwhile Matt wasn't always in the best of health, which must have made it harder for him to tackle the George Best conundrum, and if possible he didn't want to do anything to disrupt the incredible talent which George brought to the team.*

▼ Taking advantage of an opening which no ordinary footballer would have even perceived, Best's goal against Spurs in February 1971 was a flash of sheer inspiration. Manchester United were at home on the thirteenth anniversary of the Munich air disaster when a high cross from the right was delivered into the Londoners' penalty box and a defender misheaded, so that the ball steepled vertically and dropped towards the brilliant Irish goalkeeper Pat Jennings.

With the Reds' robust front-runner Alan Gowling buzzing around dangerously in front of him, the advancing Jennings could manage only a misdirected punch, diverting the bouncing ball to the feet of George Best, some 12 yards out and to the left of the goal. There were no fewer than five opponents between the little magician and the net but he didn't hesitate, lobbing the ball in the gentlest of arcs over the Spurs contingent and into the far corner of the goal. What made it so astonishing was that there were three men – Jennings, Phil Beal (number six) and Peter Collins – stationed on the line, but so perfect was George's touch that they were helpless to intervene. His euphoric reception of the applause suggested his instant realisation that he had defied all laws of probability, and he wanted to savour the moment.

The goal came after 15 minutes to give United a lead that was soon doubled by a Willie Morgan penalty. Later Martin Peters reduced the arrears but Sir Matt Busby's team held firm thereafter to win 2–1. Still, despite the victory there was an unavoidable question over whether the side's glass was half full or half empty. On the positive side it was the eighth consecutive home win over Spurs, but against that it was the Reds' first home victory in the League for three and a half months. It was a long way from vintage Manchester United, and it was clear that Sir Matt's long-term successor would have a sizeable task on his hands.

PAT JENNINGS: *I punched the ball but I didn't quite catch it right, so I went out to try and close George down, knowing there were some lads behind me near the line. But his touch was so sure that he lifted it over all of us. There was a little bit of luck involved, but the weight of his lob was perfect. It was a fantastic bit of skill, typical Bestie.*

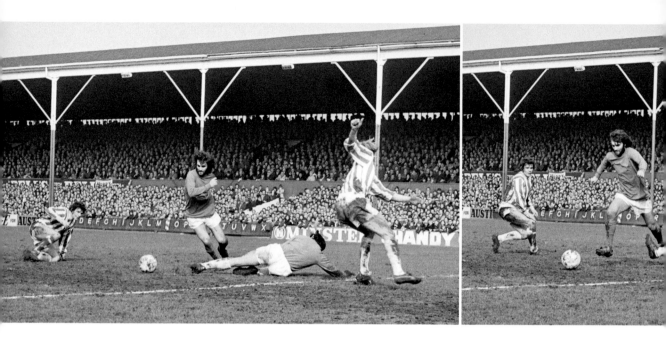

▲ There were times, plenty of them, when George Best could mesmerise an entire defence, sending his opponents twisting and swivelling in all directions while he remained balanced, focused . . . and deadly. Such an occasion was at Stoke City's Boothen End in March 1971 when he sold an outrageous dummy to wrong-foot Jackie Marsh and Alan Bloor (both out of picture), then bamboozled wing-half Eric Skeels (left), sent goalkeeper Gordon Banks plunging in an entirely unproductive direction and left both rugged centre-half Denis Smith (right) and full-back Mike Pejic (also out of frame) not knowing whether they were coming or going.

In the second shot in the sequence these three Potters have recovered something of their collective equilibrium but not the ball, which is still at the feet of the Irishman and doing his bidding. Come the third there is resignation on the face of Skeels, horror in Banks' glance, and while Smith looked determine to intervene, even at this late stage, he didn't have a chance of preventing George from depositing the ball into the net for his second goal of the afternoon. John Ritchie replied for Stoke but United won 2–1, although not without a degree of aggravation as George was booked after a petulant spat with referee William Gow.

GORDON BANKS: *George Best was a wizard and I have always believed this goal was the finest ever scored against me. That afternoon he was unstoppable, with his incredible skills lighting up the dear old Victoria Ground like a Catherine wheel.*

He got the ball just outside our box, then teased pretty well our whole defence as he moved across the pitch looking for a way to break through. He was all dummies and drag-backs, and our lads, who were all terrific players, hardly knew which way to turn. They were having to twist every which way you could imagine – it was as though someone had just put a Chubby Checker record on the public address system!

It was astonishing because he kept showing that much of the ball that I was certain he would lose it, but every time a tackle came in he was gone with it. Suddenly he was face to face with me, I could practically see the whites of his eyes, and there was nothing left for me to do but to charge out in an attempt to cut down his angle. I knew I must keep my eyes on the ball rather than on George, and I did that, but still he managed twice to send me the wrong way before, with one last drop of his shoulder, he left me sitting on my backside in the mud.

All that remained was for him to pop the ball into the net and when he did it, even though it was a close game and our fans were desperate for us to win, the whole ground burst into spontaneous applause. That was only fitting because they had just witnessed something truly special. I wouldn't have thought it possible for any foot-baller to mesmerise so many opponents in such a small space. He shook off five high-quality defenders in much the same way a dog might shake the water off his back. The great Sir Stanley Matthews, who was watching from the stands, summed it up perfectly after the match when he said: 'Stoke one, George Best two.'

12

A SEISMIC CONVULSION
1971/72

12
A SEISMIC CONVULSION
1971/72

Having the shirt pulled off his back was all in an afternoon's work for George Best, who routinely faced far more physically damaging attacks than the one served up by Fulham left-back Fred Callaghan in Manchester United's 2–1 pre-season friendly defeat at Craven Cottage in August 1971 (opposite).

The game was the outset of the first campaign under new manager Frank O'Farrell, who had been recruited from Leicester City and whose appointment signalled the failure of Sir Matt Busby's strategy of keeping the job within the United 'family'. By investing in O'Farrell's predecessor Wilf McGuinness, United had pursued a policy which was to bear rich dividends for Liverpool following the reign of their own Busby equivalent, Bill Shankly.

The Anfield succession, comprising Bob Paisley, Joe Fagan and Kenny Dalglish, had brought unprecedented glory to Merseyside and that was the vision Busby nursed for Old Trafford. One problem was that the worthy McGuinness, at 31, wasn't quite ready for the colossal responsibility thrust on him, unlike Paisley, who was a mature character in his mid-fifties when he assumed charge of Liverpool.

But there were other difficulties, too. Where Paisley inherited a high-quality squad containing top footballers who had yet to peak, McGuinness had infinitely less bountiful resources, with the notable exception of Best. There was also the fact that the man who followed Shankly was given money to spend and, crucially, that his predecessor did not remain at the club, looking over his shoulder and possibly proving a psychological burden.

Whatever the truth of that, O'Farrell came in with a clean slate, a man of unimpeachable integrity and with a record of relatively modest but well-organised success with Weymouth, Torquay United and, most recently, Leicester City, whom he had just led to the Second Division championship.

There was an overpowering element of pantomime about George Best's first sending off in domestic football, which happened at Stamford Bridge in only the second game of Frank O'Farrell's brief but incident-packed managerial tenure. The Irishman was dismissed by referee Norman Burtenshaw for foul and abusive language which, in the heat of the action, the official believed had been directed at him. George maintained stoutly that his offensive remark – 'You're a f****** disgrace' – was addressed not to the man in black but to his teammate Willie Morgan, who supported the Irishman's version of events at the disciplinary hearing which followed. Years later the episode took on an even

George, looking utterly dumbfounded at being ordered from the pitch at Stamford Bridge, in the second League game under Frank O'Farrell, is ushered away by full-back Tony Dunne, an eminently sensible character, and Bobby Charlton, whose pained expression perhaps reveals plenty about his true feelings over Best's behaviour.

more farcical tinge when Best declared that he had, in fact, been swearing at Burtenshaw, and that Morgan had been no more than a convenient alibi, one which observers found wholly believable because there was little love lost between George and Willie.

The Chelsea contretemps, coming as it did in the first half and with the hosts already a goal to the good, might have been expected to cost United dearly on the day, but they rallied magnificently in the second period to win 3–2, thanks to a header from Brian Kidd, a Willie Morgan penalty and a typically explosive finish from Bobby Charlton.

The men sitting in judgement at the FA disciplinary hearing into Best's dismissal at Stamford Bridge accepted the player's story that he intended to rebuke his teammate rather than the referee. No doubt O'Farrell would have believed George's story at the time, because there is no way he would have been involved in subterfuge.

George Best and his new manager might have hailed from different planets, so contrasting were their approaches to life when they got to know each other in the summer of 1971. George was the freewheeling, serially unpunctual but, deep down, frustrated superstar, representing the emerging breed of pop-idol footballers, and Frank was a

Besieged by the press, Frank O'Farrell leads George Best and star witness Willie Morgan from the FA hearing.

traditional, impeccably reliable, somewhat sober-sided adherent to the old school, a man who would never shirk a responsibility or fail to do his duty in any circumstance.

The outcome of the hearing was a considerable relief because Best had a six-week suspended ban hanging over his head, and if he had been found guilty of bad-mouthing Burtenshaw there had been speculation that he might be sidelined for three months. In his fragile state of mind, such a sentence might have driven him away from the game, although he was destined to depart Old Trafford soon enough anyway.

As he wrote around that time: 'I must confess, just recently football has become too much like work for me. This is because at the back of my mind I have been nagged by the thought that we just could not win anything.' On a practical level, such cogitations revealed an atrocious attitude, but also the depth of his personal frustration, as well as highlighting the scale of the task facing the unfortunate O'Farrell. He did his best, though maybe he was not an expansive enough character to manage Manchester United. He never quite convinced the majority of the players that he was the right man for the job, as reflected by Denis Law's succinct summing up: 'Frank O'Farrell came as a stranger, and he left as a stranger.'

▲ It was not all agony for Manchester United and George Best during the reign of Frank O'Farrell. Indeed, only a month after his dismissal at Stamford Bridge, the Red Devils' mercurial number 11 was scoring a thrilling hat-trick in the 4–2 defeat of West Ham at Old Trafford, and the team was bowling along merrily near the top of the First Division table. This tableau from the mid-September visit of the Hammers depicts the second of his three strikes and offers a telling illustration of his capabilities.

Bobby Charlton had taken a corner on the right, the ball had been misheaded by a West Ham defender, then it glanced off the flaxen topknot of Denis Law towards George, who was lurking just outside the six-yard box. As it came to him he was facing away from goal, but he swivelled to make space in one fluid movement and volleyed first time into the left-hand corner of the net, all while losing his balance and falling on his backside. It was a piece of stunning opportunism while hemmed in by three opponents, left to right, Geoff Hurst, Frank Lampard and Billy Bonds, while United teammates Alan Gowling (number four) and Law are on hand in case of a rebound.

George's first goal that afternoon was a routine nod from another Charlton corner and his third also stemmed from the quadrant, equalling the second for verve and ingenuity and affording him particular pleasure because it involved the gulling of one of his most respected opponents, England's World Cup-winning captain Bobby Moore. That time Best received the ball wide on the left and cut inside past befuddled right-back John Mc-Dowell, shaping to shoot as Moore threw himself forward in an attempt to block the ball.

DAVID SADLER: *By the early 1970s, under Frank O'Farrell, George was carrying the team, all the way to the top of the League for a while. With the team falling apart, he became the team, and it must have been frustrating for him, to put it mildly.*

George had seen him coming, though, checking, then instantly whipping the ball to the side before scoring with a precise shot across goalkeeper Bobby Ferguson. It was a moment which offered particular pleasure as Moore was renowned for jockeying attackers instead of committing himself to rash tackles. This time he gambled and lost, which gave Best a surge of sheer exhilaration, and the Irishman admitted many years later that if he could have experienced moments like that every week then premature retirement would never have entered his mind.

Yet for all the flair of that performance, which gave United their sixth win in eight League games, there were respected critics who maintained staunchly that O'Farrell's team was not a good one and that a dismal slump was only a matter of time. Numbered among them were Brian Clough, boss of the Derby County side which would finish the season as champions, and the flamboyant Malcolm Allison, whose Manchester City would come fourth, albeit only a point adrift of the title-winning Rams.

On *The Big Match*, ITV's much-loved Sunday afternoon football highlights show, the pair of them were unsparing in their criticism of United, although the host, the splendid Brian Moore, signed off with a montage of Best's hat-trick and the good-natured quip: 'If Manchester United are a bad team, they have a funny way of showing it.' Messrs Clough and Allison, however, would have the last laugh.

▶ George Best was in particularly scintillating form in the 4–2 victory over West Ham, as poor Frank Lampard – the father of the Chelsea and England midfielder of the same name – discovered to his cost. Typically the Irishman would feint to go outside his opponent, then cut inside, but he was quite capable of darting either way, such was his remarkable balance and immaculate technique on the ball.

Lampard was one of the finest full-backs in the land, but even he was tricked into committing himself to a challenge as the swaying Best was about to disappear in the opposite direction, leaving him stranded and, for the moment, out of the game. The haunted look on the defender's face told the story more eloquently than any words.

▲ With every respect to Sheffield United, it's unlikely that even their most enthusiastic fan would have dreamed at the start of the campaign that after ten games they would be top of the table, having recorded eight victories and two draws. But so it was, and the man who finally burst their bubble, at Old Trafford on a blazing sunny Saturday in mid-autumn, was George Best.

Frank O'Farrell's men, who had also made a buoyant start to the season with six wins and only one defeat, had huffed and puffed for most of the afternoon, but after some 85 minutes the combined efforts of Best, Law, Charlton *et al.* had failed to engineer a breakthrough, and it looked for all the world as if the visitors would re-cross the Pennines unvanquished.

Then Alex Stepney took a goal-kick at the Stretford End, the ball was nodded on by Brian Kidd and it fell to Best, who had found space just outside and to the left of the centre circle inside Sheffield United's half. He controlled the ball, then appeared to pause for thought as he gazed around him. Was he looking for a passing option? If so, he dismissed the notion immediately and suddenly set off running diagonally towards the right side of the Blades' goal.

There were massed ranks of defenders in front of him, intent on claiming an honourable point, and George was driven wide as he accelerated with apparently effortless poise past three direct challenges, leaving several other would-be tacklers unable even to get close. It might have been an optical illusion, but as he sprinted he seemed to move faster and faster as the markers fell away, unable to intervene. Finally, as he was approaching the right corner of the six-yard box, he clipped a perfectly placed cross-shot which curled just inside the far post. The deadlock had been broken and George Best had scored one of his most vividly memorable goals.

All at once John Harris's team, so long content to claim a resolute draw, now sprang forward in the desperate hope of a late equaliser and in doing so they left themselves open at the back, allowing Alan Gowling to make it 2–0 at the death. The result lifted the Red Devils to within a point of the Blades, who declined dramatically in subsequent months, eventually finishing the season in a comparatively lacklustre tenth place in the table. It would have been scant consolation at the time but, at least with hindsight the travelling Sheffield contingent can console themselves that it took a rapier thrust from one of the world's premier talents to wreck their fabulous start to 1971/72.

▶ It was the goal of the day, one of the most spectacular efforts of the season, among the most exhilarating moments in the professional lifetime of a genius, and in the context of its lateness in a top-of-the-table encounter, then it was crucial indeed. Small wonder, then, that George Best should be gathered in and hugged by Bobby Charlton, who knew a thing or two about dramatic interventions himself.

At this moment, too, Frank O'Farrell's star was in the ascendancy, and although there was no shortage of pundits who declared that his team was being carried by Best, he was understandably

optimistic. To be precise, although George was playing like a young god, he wasn't actually carrying the team completely – after all, it did still contain Law and Charlton who, although declining inevitably with the passing of years, still had quality to offer. Also there were the admirable likes of goalkeeper Alex Stepney, defenders Tony Dunne and David Sadler, and thrusting young attacker Brian Kidd, while at this early stage of the season one-time winger Willie Morgan and former centre-forward Alan Gowling were making a creditable stab at their new jobs in midfield.

Manchester United fans exulted wildly and savoured dreams of renewed title glory. Alas, they were living in a fools' paradise. Dark days were not far away.

▲ For all the inevitable concentration on George Best's unique brilliance with the ball at his feet, he was always one of the most industrious footballers in the League, too, relishing the process of pushing himself to his physical limits. But never was he in quite such perpetual motion as at Newcastle on 23 October 1971 and, distressingly, the reason had nothing to do with the game. What made him never stop running that day at St James' Park was that he had received a death threat from someone purporting to represent the IRA and was determined to make himself as difficult a target as possible to any sniper who might have evaded the Magpies' security.

Thus it was remarkable that, despite being under such terrifying pressure, he scored the only goal of the game. Willie Morgan combined cleverly with Denis Law to set up

Brian Kidd, whose effort was parried by Newcastle keeper Iam McFaul, but only into the path of the constantly mobile Best, who smashed the rebound past his Irish international teammate's despairing dive. As it turned out, the crank who issued the warning to George that his life was on the line – and George was convinced that it was a crank, despite taking every precaution – had done the Reds a favour, because the Irishman was even more of a nightmare to mark than ever, and he was never easy.

Still, it was hardly a pleasant experience, having his home under surveillance and the team coach checked for explosives, arriving at the ground flanked by bodyguards, then cringing as he took in the blocks of high-rise flats overlooking the stadium, reflecting that they must contain plenty of vantage points for any would-be assassins.

The unsettling situation was believed to have been caused by rumours circulating in Belfast that George, who had a Protestant upbringing but was never remotely political, had made a substantial donation to the controversial Democratic Unionist Party leader Ian Paisley. He was frightened as much for his family as himself, but was determined not to miss the game for fear of creating a precedent. After all, if he withdrew this time, what was to stop him becoming a victim of repeated hoaxes? Afterwards United were given a police escort back to Manchester, while the final word was left to Newcastle boss Joe Harvey, who joked at the post-match press conference: 'I wish they had shot the little bugger!'

Sadly the stress continued, with the *Manchester Evening News* being warned that if George played for Northern Ireland in the forthcoming European Championship qualifier against Spain in Belfast then he might never return to England. This time he did pull out of the game, which was subsequently postponed and played at Hull's Boothferry Park in the following February, with George performing creditably in a 1–1 draw.

However, such traumatic distractions came at a difficult time for the Irishman, who was deeply dissatisfied with his footballing lot and turning increasingly to drink. The downward spiral was emphatically under way.

Aside from Alex Stepney, George Best was the top goalkeeper in the Manchester United team and there was little he loved better in training than a session between the posts. The goal may have seemed vast with only such a diminutive figure in front of it (overleaf), but George was a natural athlete and invariably he gave an impressive account of himself. He relished the challenge and the temporary escape from the reality of opponents hacking away at his legs, though his old chum David Sadler was convinced he would have

excelled in any position. 'When you watched him tackling and heading and passing and running into position, you just knew there was nobody better at playing football in any area of the pitch. George would have been brilliant wherever any manager asked him to play.'

PADDY CRERAND: *He loved playing in goal. Lots of great players love that. Bobby Charlton did. Wayne Rooney does.*

Best coped with a sustained assault on his person throughout his decade in the Manchester United first team, and the batterings seemed increasingly concentrated as he became ever more the focal point of the side due to the gradual decrease in influence of his ageing fellow geniuses Bobby Charlton and Denis Law.

As United rode high in the first flush of Frank O'Farrell's management in the autumn on 1971, Best enjoyed a run of 11 goals in as many games while his colleagues contributed a total of seven, which is not to say United were a one-man team but certainly it highlighted to opponents who was the most important individual to stop.

George rounded off November in regal fashion, with his second hat-trick of the campaign in a 5–2 demolition of Southampton at the Dell, and when United beat Nottingham Forest 3–2 at Old Trafford on December 4 they were five points clear of nearest rivals Derby County, Manchester City and Leeds with practically half the season gone.

Operating under typically severe physical pressure, just ahead of a crunching tackle from behind by Middlesbrough full-back John Craggs, George Best maintains his poise while retaining perfect control of the football.

But then the rot long-predicted by Clough, Allison and the rest set in with a vengeance. The Reds were swept comprehensively from title contention through a ruinous run which began with three straight draws in the rest of December, then continued into 1972 with seven successive defeats. George's apprehension that he was propping up an essentially poor team took fearful shape with the 3–0 reverse at West Ham on New Year's Eve and he reacted by running away from his problem while seeking solace in alcohol.

For some time his punctuality for training sessions had been unreliable, causing resentment among some of his teammates, but now he absented himself for a week while tales of his tempestuous social life were all over newspaper columns and television bulletins. It was a seismic convulsion which amounted to the first comprehensive public demonstration of the mess his life was in. Duly Frank O'Farrell fined him two weeks' pay, ordered extra training sessions in the afternoons and cancelled his days off for the next five weeks. In addition the manager commanded him to leave the luxury home he'd had built in Bramhall – which had become both the focus of his excesses and a destination for rubber-necking fans – and return to his digs with Mrs Fullaway at her council house in Chorlton-cum-Hardy.

He missed the next game, a gruesome 3–1 home defeat by Wolves, before returning for the remainder of the season in which, despite all the travail, he contributed another nine goals in League and FA Cup. That made him twice as prolific as any teammate and was the second highest total in his career (26), so at this stage, purely in footballing terms, there was still plenty to cling to.

United's post-Christmas slump had seen them drop from leadership in the title race to eighth place, but with O'Farrell having made two splendid springtime signings – the dashing attacker Ian Storey-Moore from Nottingham Forest and Martin Buchan, the magnificent young Aberdeen defender and recent Scottish footballer of the year – there were reasonable grounds for hope among the Old Trafford faithful.

However, the festering sore of the George Best situation which had done so much to undermine O'Farrell's efforts was about to deteriorate into something which, in terms of the 26-year-old star's United future, became the penultimate stage of a terminal illness.

In the spring of 1971, Nobby Stiles was transferred to Middlesbrough as a 29-year-old. George and Nobby had known their happiest and most fruitful days at Old Trafford together, and when the England World Cup hero and veteran of numerous Manchester

Something doesn't seem quite right here. The fiendishly snarling figure at George Best's heels, baring his famous fangs as he moves in for what he intends to be the kill, is none other than Nobby Stiles.

United triumphs left the team, a significant chunk of the Red Devils' passion, commitment and very heart drained away.

In fact, Nobby was sold only because injuries had severely reduced his capacity for the earth-jarring challenges that became his trademark, though he was not missed merely for his muscle, but also for his acutely intelligent reading of the action on which his entire game was based.

Thanks to countless training sessions together, Stiles was all too aware of how difficult George would be to catch when he faced him during an FA Cup fifth round replay at Ayresome Park in February 1972. He was difficult to keep up with when Nobby was fully fit, and the job was ten times more difficult now the defender was struggling physically.

United ran out comfortable 3–0 victors thanks to a penalty from Willie Morgan and strikes by Best and Bobby Charlton, though they had found it considerably harder in the first match at Old Trafford three days earlier, when Nobby had been given an appropriately affectionate reception by the home fans who would always love him.

Pure theatre – the star, the ball and the crowd. It was April Fool's Day 1972 and, though nobody realised at the time, George Best was parading his skills at Coventry towards the end of what was to prove his last full campaign as a Manchester United player. On this day he contributed a raking long-range effort to a 3–2 victory and, despite the troubles which had engulfed him, he finished as the Reds' leading scorer for the fifth season in succession.

13

BREAKING POINT
1972/73 – 1973/74

13
BREAKING POINT
1972/73 – 1973/74

Shortly before his twenty-sixth birthday, George announced his retirement from the game in May 1972, also admitting that he was getting through a bottle of spirits every day. 'Mentally I'm a bloody wreck and I'm finished with football,' he told a battalion of pressmen as the sun beat down and the drinks flowed. With one foot on the ball and the other on his suitcase, a glass of champagne in his hand, he looks desperately disconsolate, a lost boy who has taken the wrong turning in life but can do nothing to rectify the sorry situation.

After scoring for Manchester United in their 3–0 home victory over Stoke City on the last day of the domestic campaign, he should have joined up with Northern Ireland for the home

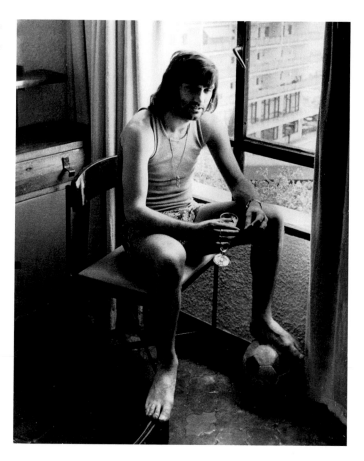

A posed picture, no doubt, but this shot of George Best in sombre mood in his hotel room in Marbella in May 1972 rings poignantly true.

internationals, but instead he headed for Spain and drank copiously. The announcement of his retirement followed, and there were plenty of pictures of George looking cool and jaunty on the beach and beside the pool, but most of his genuine footballing friends feared for him, and with good reason. The truth was that he was horrendously mixed up, debilitated by alcohol, utterly confused.

There followed a summer of speculative news stories – would he or wouldn't he return to the game? – before he declared a week into July that he would resume his career with United after all. The club welcomed him back but suspended him for two weeks and told him to live with Paddy Crerand and his family, an arrangement which seemed unlikely to last very long. As his fellow European Cup winner put it: 'It was never going to work out, looking after someone who was as worldly wise as George was by that time. Anyway, I think my kids drove him bonkers.' In a few days he had moved out.

However, the good news for fans who yearned for the great player he had once been was that he was aiming to be in the team for the start of the new season. And so he was, but for them, for George and for anyone who cared about true excellence in sport, disillusionment was lying in wait.

▶ Denis Law and George Best must surely have cringed had they realised what was in store for themselves and their club as they mulled over the imminent 1972/73 campaign at the Old Trafford pre-season photocall. Manchester United would find themselves up to their ears in the relegation mire, manager Frank O'Farrell would be summarily sacked, Denis would be discarded callously by new boss Tommy Docherty and George . . . oh dear, George!

On a positive note, the spanking new shirts looked terrific, with the pure, deep red decorated with nothing but the club badge. However, it did offer a worrying nod towards the rapacious modern trend of frequent kit changes. Throughout the 1960s and into the next decade the shirt had barely altered at all, then for 1971/72 the collars and white vees were added, with this crested version being introduced only a season later.

At the time the new shirts didn't equate to pound signs in the eyes of marketing men desperate to push their brand. In fact, back in the early 1970s there were barely any marketing men, there was no brand, and certainly there were no 'customers', as fans are often termed today. Archaic though it sounds in 2012, all that resided at Old Trafford was a football club.

▶ George Best turned on the style against Leicester City at Filbert Street in November 1972, dancing over the ball with the flamboyance of a toreador. However, although he scored United's opener in a 2–2 draw between two teams toiling in the wrong half of the First Division table – painful enough for the Foxes, hitherto unthinkable for the Red Devils – the Irishman was nowhere near premium form and, in retrospect, it is hardly surprising that it proved to be the final goal of his penultimate season with the Old Trafford institution.

With Best's behaviour becoming increasingly erratic – he snubbed Bobby Charlton's September testimonial as relations between the two men had become temporarily less than cordial – he began the term as a labouring, less-than-fully-fit member of a frankly dreadful team. United lost their first three matches and didn't win until their tenth, by which time the unfortunate O'Farrell was under severe pressure.

In October he made headlines by paying a then-astronomical £200,000 to sign prolific Third Division marksman Ted MacDougall from Bournemouth, and the opportunistic Scot gave grounds for optimism by supplying the winner against Birmingham City on his Old Trafford debut. But with only four victories secured by late November, and with deep misgivings about his own contribution, George was at breaking point.

After being fined for skipping training, he was dropped and transfer-listed in early December, and was still sidelined in mid-month when United, their football ever more wretched, plunged to a mortifying 5–0 defeat at Crystal Palace. Now the Reds were in truly calamitous straits and the inevitable upshot was the sacking of O'Farrell, who was axed at the same board meeting that accepted a retirement letter from George Best.

It was a harrowing epistle which had clearly demanded a deal of searingly distressing soul-searching on the part of the tormented Irishman. It read:

I had thought seriously of coming personally and asking for a chance to speak at the board meeting, but once again, I am afraid, when it came to saying things face to face I might not have been completely honest. I am afraid, through my somewhat unorthodox ways of trying to sort my own problems out, I have caused Manchester United even bigger problems . . . when I said last summer I was going to quit football, contrary to what many people said or thought, I seriously meant it, because I had lost interest in the game for various reasons.

While in Spain I received a lot of letters from both friends and well-wishers, quite a few asking me to reconsider. I did so and after weeks of thinking it over I decided to give it another try. It was an even harder decision to make than the original one. I came back hoping that my appetite for the game would return, and even though in every game I like to think I gave one hundred per-cent, there was something missing. Even now I am not quite sure what.

Therefore I have decided not to play football again and this time no one will change my mind. In conclusion I would like to wish the club the best of luck for the remainder of the season and for the future. Because even though I personally have tarnished the club's name in recent times, to me and thousands of others, Manchester United still means something special.

For all his antics, and the grief they had caused, it took a hard heart not to feel at least a shred of sympathy for a young man of unique abilities who had lost his way. O'Farrell, too, deserved some compassion, particularly as Sir Matt Busby and chairman Louis Edwards were said to have been dealing with George behind his back while he was at his wits' end as he strove to revive his moribund team. Clearly his job had been rendered immeasurably more difficult by the Best situation, and now he left the club an inconsolably bitter man.

Meanwhile Blackpool waxworks melted down their model of George Best, who became involved in a number of non-football-related scrapes, travelled to Toronto, Los Angeles, Palm Springs and Acapulco, sold the boutiques that he had owned, took a holiday in Spain . . . and continued to drink heavily.

Meanwhile back at Old Trafford, it was all happening. With George in the throes of quasi-retirement once more, Manchester United had appointed the colourful, controversial Tommy Docherty as Frank O'Farrell's successor and, after bolstering the team with a legion of his fellow Scots – described by the tabloids as 'Doc's Tartan Army' – he had averted the unthinkable nightmare of demotion to the second tier, an indignity which the Red Devils had not suffered since the Second World War.

A week or two after United's (temporary) salvation had been achieved, George faced a new crisis of his own, one which might have cost him his life. While vacationing in Marbella his leg became grotesquely swollen and painful, a local doctor proved unable to help and he flew home in agony. A thrombosis was diagnosed and he was rushed to hospital in Manchester, where he was treated successfully. Soon he was visited by none other than Sir Matt Busby – the pair had a pleasant chat and then, as the most influential figure in the Irishman's adult life was leaving, he delivered the throwaway line: 'Isn't it about time you were playing again?'

That simple question affected George profoundly. Repeatedly he had pondered an-

other comeback but couldn't make up his mind. Now, knowing that he was wanted by the man he respected more than any other in the game, his course was clear. Later he explained: 'The longer I stayed away the harder it got. I hadn't even had the nerve to go to Old Trafford to watch any matches. But then I met some of the players socially, they were tremendous and almost every one of them asked me to come back again. All sorts of people kept asking me . . . it made me feel good and I plucked up courage to ring manager Tommy Docherty. I was delighted with the way he spoke to me and we arranged a meeting.'

Thus embraced by the Doc (opposite), the prodigal returned in September, seriously overweight and with shirt buttons straining after some nine months away from football, but professing himself ready to work like a Trojan, afternoons as well as mornings, in a bid to rehabilitate himself. Still only 27, he was afire with enthusiasm and he knuckled down. He knew it would be a lengthy process but, with United again playing like drains, Docherty was eager for his inspiration and on October 20 George found himself being thrown in at the First Division deep end. What happened next wasn't particularly pretty.

DAVID SADLER: *When George came back under Tommy Docherty, although he had declined a long way from his peak, he was still better than anything else United had got. So his friends in the dressing room hoped against hope that he could regain some of the old magic to improve what had become a poor side. Sadly, it wasn't to be.*

▶ To say the Old Trafford faithful were desperate for some sort, any sort, of messiah in the autumn of 1973 was the understatement of the season, and when a slightly portly George Best ambled out of the tunnel to face Birmingham City one misty afternoon, he was greeted by a wave of thunderous adulation the like of which the old ground had not known for five years or more.

Expectation was at fever pitch and, inevitably and understandably, George was unable to meet it. But although he was a shadow of his former self, there were enough encouraging touches – his capacity for deft flicks and cleverly angled

passes had clearly not diminished – to massage the hope that, given a run of games to regain his equilibrium and hone his fitness, the Irishman could still make a colossal contribution to the Reds' revival plans.

That day he was exhausted long before the end and replaced by substitute Mick Martin, so he wasn't on the field when United scored the only goal of the game, the sorely needed victory being only their fourth in a dozen League outings. What highlighted their plight most vividly was the astonishing circumstance that their winner was stroked home from the penalty spot by goalkeeper Alex Stepney – and if that was not surreal enough in itself, what about the fact that it made him the club's current leading marksman, along with Brian Kidd and Sammy McIlroy, on a mere two goals?

Still, in the weeks that followed George demonstrated a serious intention to improve, scoring at Tottenham in November and at home to Coventry City in December, but there were no more wins until after Christmas and the optimism generated by the Irishman's return had pretty well dissipated by the turn of the year. All that remained now was the last depressing act of George Best's Manchester United career.

▶ For all those with Manchester United's interests at heart, New Year's Day 1974 could hardly have been more miserable. Already distressingly near to the foot of the table, the Red Devils played pitiably in a 3–0 defeat by Queen's Park Rangers at Loftus Road which would have been far more comprehensive but for Alex Stepney's defiant excellence between the sticks.

Making his twelfth consecutive appearance since his comeback, George Best lasted the whole 90 minutes and was by no means the most wretched performer on show, but only rarely did he ruffle his classy marker Dave Clement and when he walked off the pitch at the finish he was despondent. That evening he decided he needed a party to cheer himself up and threw himself into what remained of the seasonal festivities with such gusto that he missed the first two days back at training. The upshot was that Docherty axed him from the next weekend's FA Cup tie with Plymouth Argyle, suspended him and placed him on the transfer list. George Best never played another competitive game for Manchester United, who were deservedly relegated at season's end.

At the time he told David Meek of the *Manchester Evening News* that he was finished with League football for good: 'The reason is simple. I know now that I have lost forever that certain spark that set me apart from other players and I also know that I can never get it back. I said when I returned to Manchester United that if I could not recapture my

previous form I would call it a day. I am just sticking by that promise.'

Meek asked him if United's sorry state had any bearing on his retirement at the age of 27: 'Perhaps it helped to make the decision easier, but it was not the main reason. I think even if I had been with Leeds United [then the top team in the country] I still would have quit. I still believe I am a good First Division player, but I have to be better than that to continue. In the past I enjoyed being that little bit special – who wouldn't? I could not face being just an average First Division player.'

So there it was. Manchester United had been demoted from the top flight for the first time since 1937 and been finally abandoned by arguably their greatest ever footballer, all in the same season.

PAT JENNINGS: *Having done so much towards Manchester United winning the European Cup, understandably enough George wanted to play at that level every year. But United were falling away rather than getting better, and I know that frustrated him. I'd have thought he'd have gone on much longer with United if they'd had a better side in the early 1970s.*

DAVID SADLER: *Towards the end of his time at United, when he was drinking heavily, maybe some of his friends, including myself, could have done more to try and talk him round. But that's with the benefit of more than 40 years of hindsight. Back then we were all mainly looking after our own careers.*

14

THE PRIDE AND THE FRUSTRATION
1964 – 1977

14
THE PRIDE AND
THE FRUSTRATION
1964 – 1977

George Best loved his country. He was proud to be Irish and to wear the green shirt. But – and it's a big, sad, overwhelming but – he was monumentally frustrated by his experience of international football. His problem was that the Northern Ireland team wasn't remotely good enough during his era to qualify for major tournaments, so that no matter how magnificent his own contribution might prove, invariably his colleagues would let him down. Sometimes George would dazzle as only he could, but the others couldn't capitalise on his brilliance, repeatedly missing goal-scoring opportunities he had fashioned, not giving him the ball at the right time, or failing to read the subtle intentions behind his passing.

In the early days of his career, he felt it almost surreal when switching from the flair, quality and relentless ambition of Manchester United to the comparatively humble scuffling of the Irish set-up. He enjoyed the camaraderie of international get-togethers, and he tried his utmost both in training and in games, but increasingly he saw it as a time to have a laugh with some old mates, almost a holiday from his main job – hence his scathing description of the process as 'recreational football'.

It wasn't that he was big-headed, and he acknowledged that the likes of Pat Jennings, Derek Dougan and Johnny Crossan were completely at home at the top level, but the squad desperately needed more such talented individuals if the Ulstermen were ever to make a telling impact.

How George envied Old Trafford teammates Bobby Charlton and Nobby Stiles when they went away to join England. They travelled with the expectation of genuine achievement, of winning the game's premier prizes, while he knew, in his heart, that a Northern Ireland side containing yeomen from the lower divisions, and occasionally even part-timers, just was not equipped for the real battle.

Frequently he was dubbed one of the finest players on the planet, which was all very well, but he yearned for the opportunity to prove it in World Cups and European Championships, to let his ability be judged alongside the great men to whom he was constantly compared, the Pelés, the Eusebios and the Cruyffs.

Might he have retained his equilibrium, and therefore lengthened his career, had he been granted the fulfilment of top-rank international football? Dougan, for one, was in no doubt, putting it like this: 'If George had been born an Englishman, he would have excited the world.'

The word 'tragedy' can be employed legitimately to describe what happened to the Irishman in the second half of his life, so it might seem glib to use such an extreme description when discussing mere footballing disappointments. But in a strictly sporting context it was just that, a tragedy, that George Best's birthplace prevented him from showcasing his lustrous gifts on the grandest of stages, and that he collected only 37 caps, instead of three times that number. For the sake of comparison, his pal Jennings made a record 119 appearances for his country, not vacating the international stage until 1982.

PAT JENNINGS: *He was criticised sometimes for not playing, but he would never have missed an opportunity to represent his country if he'd been fit. As it was he often turned out when carrying bad injuries that would have sidelined most people. George loved playing for Northern Ireland and it was a pleasure to be in the team with him. Certainly, whenever he did appear our spirits would rise because we knew we could win any game if he was there.*

Our international debut against Wales was a huge occasion for both George and myself, and I think we helped each other through it. We were the two youngest in the squad so it made sense for us to room together, and that was the start of a lasting friendship. We were both quiet lads, neither of us had a lot to say and we got on brilliantly. He was always the same George Best, he never changed, he never wanted special treatment or put on airs and graces, even when he had made his name as one of the greatest players in the world. George was always a modest lad, and he was very clever, he always knew the answers to quiz questions about sport or films or music, or almost any subject. He was a great reader, and what he learned from the books stuck in his head.

When Manchester United's assistant manager Jimmy Murphy had mentioned Best's

George Best, on legs he might have borrowed from Bambi, tucks away the first of his nine goals for Northern Ireland in a World Cup qualifier against Switzerland in Lausanne in November 1964, his fourth full international. Sadly, but typically, the Ulstermen dropped two defensive clangers and lost 2–1.

prodigious development to an official of the Irish FA in early 1964, waxing lyrical about the rookie's ability, he had been dumbfounded when the fellow had muttered something about giving George a run-out in the youth team. 'The youth team?' rejoined United's acerbic Welshman, with a thunderously contemptuous glance. 'He's good enough for your first team and he's good enough now!'

Duly Best was called to his country's colours, made an instant impact in training sessions, and was awarded his senior debut against Wales at the Vetch Field, Swansea, in April 1964.

Though he had made only 24 appearances for United at that point, George was not overawed, contributing notably as the Irish won 3–2 and, coincidentally, facing the same direct opponent as on his club debut, Graham Williams of West Bromwich Albion. Two weeks later he sparkled in his home debut at Windsor Park, Belfast, a 3–0 victory in a so-called friendly against Uruguay in which the right-back attempted, in vain, to intimidate him with a series of violent tackles. Thereafter George Best was a fixture in the Irish side, whenever he was available.

Totally self-possessed and eager to express himself in his first game at Wembley, against England in November 1965, George Best tormented the defenders who were destined to become world champions only eight months later on that same stretch of turf. The precocious 19-year-old is deftly dragging the ball away from the impending beefy challenge of right-back George Cohen, while centre-half Jack Charlton queues up to make the next tackle.

Against England not long before their World Cup glory, George Best dazzled. Later England manager Alf Ramsey went on record as wishing that Best had been born an Englishman, and the Manchester United man's performance in this game would have done plenty to strengthen that fruitless yen. The game finished 2–1 to the hosts, but not before George had shown just how hard he was to pin down by nipping away from England captain Bobby Moore to set up an equaliser for Willie Irvine. Joe Baker had opened the scoring and Alan Peacock notched the winner, but it was Best who riveted the eye as he gave his markers a torrid time. Sadly, and this would become an all-too-familiar story, the other wearers of the green shirt were unable to capitalise on his exceptional approach play.

▶ Best's performance at a boggy Windsor Park, Belfast, in October 1967 was, unquestionably, the *tour de force* of his international career. He didn't score the goal which defeated

Scotland, but he created it with his heady cocktail of dash, daring and wizardry – and throughout an afternoon in which his home-town crowd basked in the glory of his opulent gifts, the boy from across the city in Burren Way dominated the proceedings with an utter certainty of purpose and execution not witnessed before or since on Irish turf.

To put his achievement in due context, it should be noted that this Scotland side saw themselves as global champions after defeating England, the holders of the World Cup, only six months earlier. Among the visitors was Denis Law, George's Manchester United comrade and a world-class footballer by any reckoning, and even he had to concede the stage to the maestro in the green shirt.

Captivating the crowd with his sinuous dribbles from every quarter of the pitch, engineering holes in the Scottish rearguard seemingly at will and gulling befuddled opponents into kicking at thin air, Best ran them so ragged that his principal marker, the blue-shirted number two Tommy Gemmell (right) asked Eddie McCreadie, his fellow full-back, to swap positions with him at half-time. McCreadie, who had been subjected to the full Best treatment on several occasions with Chelsea, had the admirable good sense to dismiss the request with a brisk profanity.

So if Best was so unplayable, why was the score only 1–0? The truth is that he enjoyed little meaningful help on a day in which he carried the team on his back in a manner that he would never quite be able to emulate. His teammates worked hard enough, but he was setting a celestial standard, and that despite the fact that he was hacked, body-checked and had his shirt pulled in vain attempts to suppress his artistry.

Half a dozen times he went close to scoring, which would have capped his display perfectly, but veteran Scottish keeper Ronnie Simpson kept him out with a succession of splendid saves. Astoundingly considering the one-sidedness of the contest, the decisive breakthrough was delayed until the sixty-ninth minute when George raced on to a delivery down the right touchline from full-back John Parke, then veered infield before delivering a beautifully weighted low cross for Dave Clements to sweep home past the heroic Simpson.

The *Times* put it thus: 'His genius was matched only by his courage, and he deserved the victory all on his own. He caused as much trouble as three men with some exhilarating runs and shots of quite remarkable force from such a slight frame.'

It was the only time in his international career that he really lit up the pitch in the way he did so routinely for United during his prime, yet he was modest in the wake of his masterpiece, as ever joking in the dressing room as one of the boys. Perhaps he didn't quite appreciate the enormity of his achievement at the time, but much later he described it emotionally as his game for Belfast – and that's how it passed into Irish football folklore.

PAT JENNINGS: *He didn't score that day, but he ran riot. There were players with fantastic reputations in that Scotland team, but none of them wanted to go near George because he was walking past them as if they weren't there, over and over again.*

The first truly dark moment in George Best's Northern Ireland career occurred in April 1970. The Ulstermen were a goal down to Scotland in the opening round of the home internationals and despite some frenzied pressing Billy Bingham's men just couldn't force an equaliser. With passions running dangerously high, Best moaned at referee Eric Jennings over a free-kick awarded against Irish spearhead Derek Dougan in the Scotland box, pointing out that his own shirt was being tugged constantly and that he was being kicked repeatedly.

During the course of what became an animated discussion, George placed his hand on Jennings' shoulder, which evidently wasn't a problem. But when the referee walked away, the Irishman shouted, spat and hurled a handful of mud in his direction, which could only have one result.

True, Best believed that he had been provoked beyond reason, but there was no excuse for falling out with another official only a few months after the incident with referee Jack Taylor that earned him a six-week suspension.

On this occasion, however, he got away with it in circumstances which brewed up a storm of discontent. A ban seemed inevitable but the Irish FA's international committee took the view that George had spat at the ground rather than the referee, bore in mind that he had been subjected to what they called excessive and exaggerated press criticism, and decided that the sending-off was enough punishment in itself.

This outraged the hardline English administrator Alan Hardaker, who believed the Irish had taken a lenient line in order to free their star man to play in their next game, which just happened to be against England. Not for the first time in his tempestuous career, nor the last, Hardaker pronounced himself disgusted. He dubbed the Irish action the biggest piece of hypocrisy he'd known in football, and demanded: 'How can we instil discipline in players with such an example?'

Crestfallen and looking like a drowned rat, George Best drags himself off the pitch at Windsor Park, Belfast, having been waved to the dressing room by referee Eric Jennings for throwing mud and spitting.

▲ Controversially reprieved from suspension, George Best took full advantage by plundering a wonder goal against England at Wembley three days later. Having drifted into space a few yards in from the touchline on Northern Ireland's right, he received a raking crossfield pass from Dave Clements, executed a sharp turn to leave clubmate Nobby Stiles for dead, then lost Emlyn Hughes with a sudden burst of searing acceleration before beating keeper Gordon Banks at his near post with a precisely angled low left-footer from ten yards.

It was a virtuoso effort and it equalised an earlier strike by Martin Peters, but it was rather overshadowed by the fact that Bobby Charlton was collecting his hundredth cap that evening. Bobby, skipper for the night, was only the second Englishman after Billy Wright to complete his international century, and he made doubly sure that the next day's headlines would be his by scoring near the end to complete a 3–1 England victory, Geoff Hurst having contributed the hosts' second.

Compared to Best's veritable cracker, Charlton's was a prosaic tap-in, but that was hardly going to bother Fleet Street's sports editors when England's favourite sporting son had reached such a momentous milestone.

NOBBY STILES: *I never relished playing against George because I knew exactly what he could do to defenders, having seen him so often in training as well as in games. Luckily I didn't come up against him too much when I played for England because I was in midfield, unlike for United, where I played at the back with Bill Foulkes. This goal he scored? Funny, that one seems to have slipped my mind!*

George Best bamboozles Peter Storey with a characteristic piece of startling improvisation when Northern Ireland entertained England at Windsor Park, Belfast, in May 1971.

A fair and honest player himself, George held the Arsenal tough nut Peter Storey in undisguised contempt, believing that he resorted to kicking opponents because he lacked the skill to play the game properly. Storey was one of the few men whom he delighted to taunt with his vastly superior skills, and Best revelled in the opportunity to do just this when Northern Ireland entertained England at Windsor Park, Belfast, in May 1971. 'Every time I played against him he would tell me that he was going to break my leg. I took particular pleasure in turning him inside out,' he told Joe Lovejoy, author of his excellent 1998 biography, *Bestie*.

Infuriatingly for Best, he never had the last laugh against 'Snouty' in the international arena. Though he recognised England as the ultimate scalp, he finished on the losing side in all six games he played against them, this one being decided by a single goal from Allan Clarke.

▶ One of the most hotly debated disallowed 'goals' of the age occurred during England's visit to Belfast in May 1971. The World Cup-winning goalkeeper Gordon Banks, widely recognised as the finest ever born, had the ball safely in his custody, then threw it up ready for a drop-kick down the ground.

But lurking close by was George Best, who had watched Banks in action often enough to know exactly what he was going to do. Thus he anticipated the trajectory of the ball, and raised a boot to hook it smartly away from the astonished net-minder. Now it arced behind Banks, who was helpless to prevent George from nipping round him, winning a short but desperate race to reach the bouncing ball, which he headed deftly into the empty net.

At that time attackers were allowed to harass keepers, and were entitled to play the ball when it was in the air as long as no personal contact was made. Best maintained, rightly in the view of this humble observer, that he had acted wholly within the laws of the game, but the referee didn't agree and disallowed the strike for dangerous kicking. It was a verdict that seemed spurious in the extreme as Gordon was not touched or even threatened, and there was always the point that if the keeper had kicked the ball as he intended, then his foot would have been high, too!

Insult was added to outrage for George when Northern Ireland lost the game 1–0.

GORDON BANKS: *Only two months after George had dumped me on my behind at Stoke, he attempted an even more audacious piece of opportunism against me, this time in the green shirt of Northern Ireland. It was a very tight game at Windsor Park, deep into the first half but with no goals so far, when he confronted me as I was about to punt the ball upfield after saving a shot from Eric McMordie.*

As I did my best to veer away from his challenge, I tossed the ball up ready to drop-kick it – and that's when George struck like a viper, raising a boot and nicking the ball away from me. It went behind me and as the two of us raced to catch it, he managed to nod it into the net. George thought he had scored a perfectly legal goal and the crowd went mad, but the referee gave a free-kick to England for dangerous play. I was relieved and he was furious, but most people agreed afterwards that the official had made the right decision. Certainly I was of that mind!

It got worse for George as England won 1–0 through Allan Clarke, but few people remembered that. All the football world was talking about the goal that never was, and people are still talking about it today.

PAT JENNINGS: *George did the same to me at Old Trafford once, not too long after the Gordon Banks incident. I threw the ball up, his leg came up and either my leg or his was going to be broken, so I pulled out of the challenge. I expected to be given a free-kick, just as Gordon was, but the referee had his back to the play momentarily. He saw the ball in the back of our net and he gave the goal.*

When George Best walked out on Manchester United for the last time early in 1974, it was assumed by everyone, including himself, that he would never represent Northern Ireland again. But when he began playing for Fulham in the autumn of 1976 he was recalled to the colours by the Ulstermen's new boss, the matchlessly eloquent former Tottenham Hotspur captain Danny Blanchflower, pictured here with hands in pockets alongside a slightly tubby Best during a training session.

Duly the 30-year-old George made his international comeback, having not represented Northern Ireland for nearly three years, in a World Cup qualifier against Holland in Rotterdam. Clearly he had lost a lot of his pace, but the old ingenuity remained intact and in the game, which finished 2–2 to give the visitors an extremely creditable away point, he was certainly not eclipsed, even by the sublime skills of Johan Cruyff.

Best went on to earn four more caps, his last one coming in the return with Holland, a 1–0 defeat at Windsor Park in October 1977. Five years later, when he was in his mid-thirties and playing for San Jose Earthquakes in the United States, there was talk of taking him to Spain after Northern Ireland had qualified for the World Cup finals in which they were destined to perform so valiantly, reaching the second group stage.

In truth, it was always a non-starter. Time had run out for George Best in the international arena and had he performed in Spain the world would have seen a mere travesty of the phenomenal player he had once been.

15
WHEN BESTIE MET PELÉ
1975 – 1983

15
WHEN BESTIE
MET PELÉ
1975 – 1983

More than a tad disillusioned with life, George Best sat slumped in the Maine Road dressing room ahead of his pal Mike Summerbee's testimonial match in September 1975. He wore a Manchester United shirt, and was about to play for a United European Cup Winners' XI against a City XI, but at the age of 29 he was all washed up as a United footballer, and although he relished his involvement in this tribute to Summerbee, of whom he thought the world, he might have been weighed down with the poignancy of his plight.

Having walked out of Old Trafford for good in January 1974, after a decade in which he scaled most of the club game's loftiest pinnacles before plumbing dismal personal depths, he could only look on impotently as United were relegated to the Second Division while his working life involved the running of two nightclubs.

He had been involved in a tedious and debilitating brouhaha with former Miss World Marjorie Wallace, there had been an expedition to Johannesburg for a brief but lucrative spell of games – for the Jewish Guild – and plenty of partying. He had turned out a couple of times for non-League Dunstable Town, and he had endured a steady drip-drip of unsavoury news stories. All the while his footballing future looked decidedly less than meaningful.

At this point United still controlled George Best's professional destiny, but the club finally released him from his contract on 8 November 1975 and two days later he signed with Fourth Division Stockport County to play for a month at £300 per appearance, home games only and with whatever training regime he chose.

He scored on his debut in a 3–2 win over Swansea City, his presence more than trebling the gate from just under 3,000 for the previous home match to more than 9,000 for the visit of the Welshmen, but George's Edgeley Park mission was never destined to be a lasting one.

Next on the Best horizon was an arrangement with Chelsea, which appealed far more through the twin attractions of being back in the big league and close to his now-preferred London haunts. The problem was that, in an era long before Roman Abramovich had been heard of, the Stamford Bridge club was distinctly hard up and could not meet George's demand of £1,000 per outing.

And so he turned his attention to the United States, where he believed a pot of gold to be waiting.

MIKE SUMMERBEE: *This is a sad picture because George looks so terribly alone, even in the midst of a busy dressing room. Often he grew a beard when he was going through difficulties. It was as though it was something to hide behind. There were times when he was overwhelmed by all the attention and no manager could have known how to handle the situation because it had never cropped up before.*

If you're a genius – and he was – people think you have everything, but that's not necessarily the case. I believe a lot of his problems were caused by loneliness. If he could have met the right lady at the right time and settled into a family life, I think he would have continued to enjoy a successful career for much longer. It was virtually impossible for him to have that normality because the vast majority of people he went out with were with him just because he was George Best.

▶ George Best playing for Fulham? And on a regular basis? Certainly it required a quantum leap of the imagination, and for supporters of Manchester United who had delighted in his Old Trafford pomp it would never seem palatable, but that was the inescapable reality in the autumn of 1976.

In fact, an initially influential role at Craven Cottage represented a definite step-up from George's other footballing experiences since his dog days with the Red Devils. He quite enjoyed the regular changes of scene involved in alternating between London through the winter and the United States during the English summer. With all due respect to the employers involved, fleeting engagements in Johannesburg, Dunstable and Stockport, followed by an underwhelming three-match stint with

Cork Celtic in the Republic of Ireland, killing time before an admittedly far more fulfilling season with the Los Angeles Aztecs in the North American Soccer League, added up to little more than a sporting peepshow as far as the vast majority of his former admirers were concerned.

Now, at least, he had shed the unsightly excess pounds accumulated by several years of louche living, and even if he and alcohol were not exactly strangers, he had shown enough self-discipline while training with the Aztecs in the Californian sunshine to render himself a feasible medium-term prospect for the Second Division south-west Londoners.

For 30-year-old George, given his reduced status, it was as ideal a billet as he was likely to find. He was well-paid, given a free car and flat in a location he relished and, crucially, there were some classy teammates. Holding the rearguard together was no less gilded a star than Bobby Moore, England's World Cup-winning skipper of a decade earlier, while the chief attacker was Rodney Marsh, certainly not a performer to compare with Best in his prime, but a flamboyant fellow with undeniable flair on the ball and who liked to play the game for fun.

For Fulham, at the time being managed by the gentlemanly, vastly experienced Alec Stock, it was a no-lose situation. As long as George remained on the relatively straight and narrow, he would be a fabulous crowd-puller, and if he could conjure up even a vestige of his former magic, then he would improve the team immeasurably. The Craven Cottage faithful had hardly been sated by success down the years but had enjoyed a taste of the big time when Fulham had reached the FA Cup final a year earlier and had always appreciated a dash of showbiz glamour. Now they could hardly wait for the new campaign to begin.

Red tape involved in clearing George Best's registration from Los Angeles Aztecs prevented him from taking his place in the Fulham ranks at home to Nottingham Forest on the opening day of 1976/77, but he was on parade for the fourth game of term, when Bristol Rovers visited Craven Cottage on September 4 (below).

The Irishman's presence at kick-off was clearly the principal factor in swelling the attendance

from the 9,437 who ventured forth for the 2–2 draw with Forest to the 21,127 who flocked to the picturesque Thames-side ground for the encounter with the Pirates, and he could not stand accused of wasting time before offering value for money.

A mere 71 seconds into the contest, George gave Fulham the lead with a neat finish, nothing spectacular in itself, but as an instant marker of what he might do for the Cottagers it was priceless. As the game progressed, it became increasingly evident that he had been in training and was serious about his football – on the previous page he looks as trim as the man about to tackle him, Rovers' Dave Staniforth – which laid to rest some apprehensions that his comeback was nothing more than a money-making gimmick.

There were no more goals, so George walked off at the end of 90 minutes as the match-winner, a familiar role but one he hadn't filled in an English League game for three years or more. He followed that up three days later with an audacious long-range strike in a 2–1 League Cup victory at Peterborough and the George Best show was very much back on the road.

◄ Shall we dance? Tripping the light fantastic was unlikely to be on the mind of Bristol Rovers' chief enforcer Frankie Prince as he slipped an arm around the waist of George Best during the Irishman's Fulham debut in September 1976.

Prince, a magnificent clubman who served the Pirates for more than a decade and who has been Torquay United's Football In The Community officer for the last 20 years, was under no illusions about the havoc George would wreak if he was given space, so obviously he elected to keep the tightest of reins on the Fulham debutant.

There was, however, an element of closing the stable door after the horse had bolted, as Best had sneaked away to poach what proved to be the winning goal in the second minute of the contest.

FRANKIE PRINCE: *Our manager Don Megson had given me the job of man-marking George Best, so we were both a little disappointed, shall we say, that he scored after only 71 seconds. I seem to recall it was a bit of a soft one, but it was enough to win the match. When it went in I thought to myself: 'Blimey, this could be a difficult afternoon!' But actually we did all right for the rest of the game. George was still a terrific player but as it was his first game of the season I'm not sure he was as fit as he might have been. Afterwards I had a chat and a drink with him in the bar at Craven Cottage and found him to be a very amiable fellow, with no side to him at all. It was a massive occasion for Rovers and one that I'll never forget.*

One of the positive aspects of Best joining Fulham was that he got to play alongside Rodney Marsh. The gifted duo had known each other well since Marsh turned up at Manchester City in March 1972. They got on personally, each believing in the creed of thrilling the fans with extravagant attacking football, and for a short while they entertained royally. At one point there was even talk of them making a record together, but a deal never materialised. Occasionally their antics were self-indulgent, but it was a rare Craven Cottage season ticket holder who wouldn't have excused them their odd excess for the spirit of genuine enjoyment they brought to the game.

The Georgie Best and Rodney Marsh Fulham roadshow was at full speed in the autumn of 1976 when the fashionably hirsute pair ran amok in the early going of the Second Division campaign. This time the venue was Craven Cottage, the opposition was Hereford United and the television cameras were rolling. Fulham won 4–1 to move up to fourth in the league table, with the demonstrative Marsh scoring twice and Best delighting a near-20,000 crowd with a series of stylish touches that hinted tantalisingly at the player he once was.

Sadly, it was an all-too-brief interlude before a bleak winter, results-wise, turned into a near calamitous spring. Best punctured the good-time bubble by being sent off for foully abusing a referee, Marsh suffered injury, results fell away dramatically and Alec Stock was sacked and replaced by the bluff Merseysider Bobby Campbell.

As George's satisfaction with life on the pitch declined, so did his situation away from the game. His relationship with future wife Angela Janes hit a stormy patch, he leaned more heavily on the bottle, and in February he might have been killed when, after drinking unwisely, he wrapped his chairman's daughter's car around a Knightsbridge lamp-post at four o'clock in the morning. He got away with a lattice-work of facial cuts

Rodney Marsh and George Best had lots of laughs in their fleeting interlude together at Fulham but, sadly, the good times didn't last.

and a fractured shoulder blade, missing only five games, but could do little to right the listing ship as Fulham's plummet down the Second Division left them only a point clear of the drop when the final whistle was blown in May.

Despite that, despite everything, George's 37 appearances, decorated by eight goals, were enough to win him the player of the season award, as voted for by the supporters.

Unfortunately, he was living on borrowed time at Fulham. By the start of his second term Marsh had departed, and so had the fun. After playing ten games and scoring twice for a poor team, in November 1977 he went back to Los Angeles Aztecs and the booze, never to darken the door of the Cottage dressing room again.

▶ George Best looked smart and ready for meaningful action in his crisp new Hibernian kit after signing for the Edinburgh club in November 1979. Alas, it was all a sad illusion. After scoring in his first game, a 2–1 defeat at St Mirren, he performed sketchily to put it charitably, though it was hardly surprising because Hibs were such a poor team.

Looking considerably paunchier when playing than in this posed portrait, George was badly affected by alcohol during his Easter Road stint, though that didn't stop expectant fans from pouring through the turnstiles in the vain hope that he might conjure up a flash or two of his old magic.

He did supply the goal that earned a 1–1 draw at home to top-of-the-table Celtic in January, but he was sacked in February for being too hung over to take the field for a Scottish Cup meeting with Ayr United. Hibs, who were destined to be relegated as bottom club in the top flight at season's end, were in such dire straits that they took him back. However, it was only a fleeting reprieve. He departed in April half a dozen games before season's end, having made 16 appearances and contributed three goals, and with his reputation at a new low.

Rather surprisingly George was invited back to Easter Road in 1980/81. Less remarkably, this time his presence did nothing to massage attendances and he was gone before the leaves had left the trees.

Thereafter he played only five more competitive games in British football, all for Bournemouth of the Third Division during 1982/83, but he was seriously unfit and such a travesty of his former self that it was never going to be a lasting arrangement. True, shortly before his brief tenure at Dean Court, he received an offer from Ron Atkinson, Manchester United manager at the time, to train with the team with a view to making a comeback as a Red Devil. The ever expansive – and on this occasion wildly fantasising – Atkinson suggested that George wouldn't have to do much running, but could stroll around, using his undying class to unhinge opponents with clever passes upon which his lithe young colleagues might capitalise. Mercifully for all concerned, even George, as desperate as he had become, didn't go for that one.

Back in December 1975 George had crossed the Atlantic to sign for the LA Aztecs, who plied their trade in the North American Soccer League. Later he would make much of his excitement at joining a competition which already featured the peerless Pelé and would, in time, play host to the stellar likes of Franz Beckenbauer, Johan Cruyff, Johan Neeskens and Eusebio.

However, the fact was that after a brief spurt of initial interest among American sports fans, the NASL faded into insignificance, becoming a poorly regarded backwater for mercenary ageing stars looking to cash in, understandably enough, at the end of their careers, and lower-grade performers who had struggled to survive in their own national leagues.

▶ When Pelé met Bestie . . . The brilliant Brazilian's New York Cosmos against the Irish wizard's Los Angeles Aztecs might not have been a fixture to fire the imagination of the football world, but it was a clash between two of the most talented practitioners the game had ever known and, as such, merits a modicum of attention.

Certainly the standard was not too demanding for a man of George's calibre, and he sparkled, at least in comparison with most of the men around him, as the hitherto unfancied Aztecs won a divisional championship that term. He could have signed for the Cosmos but favoured the laid-back west-coast lifestyle which, for a time, involved running a beach bar, which he named Bestie's. For a fellow of his inclinations, it was not the wisest venture he might have chosen.

In footballing terms, George Best's Stateside expedition, which extended through six summers, can be summed up concisely. He put in two seasons of decent displays with LA Aztecs (opposite), proving pivotal to the club reaching the play-offs – part of the league's convoluted trophy system – on both occasions. But then the side declined, he became dispirited and he left to join Fort Lauderdale Strikers midway through the 1978 campaign. There were some excellent players among his new teammates, notably the former Liverpool and England maestro Ian Callaghan, and George made an impressive debut, scoring with his first touch, and then again, in an unexpected 5–3 victory over New York Cosmos. Once more he played a key role in reaching the play-offs, but then suffered a worldwide ban over registration issues, fell out with coach Ron Newman, his mother died and he drank more heavily than ever.

In 1980, having spent the first part of the year with Hibs, he signed for San Jose Earthquakes, a frankly dreadful side for whom he played for two terms. His old Manchester United friend David Sadler grieved that George had become little more than a freak show, but still the enigmatic Irishman was able to produce one exquisite gem, just to nod tantalisingly at what might have been. The Earthquakes were 2–0 down to his former employers from Fort Lauderdale, when he took possession of the ball just outside the 'D' of his opponents' penalty area. Moving forward sharply, seemingly on his toes and oozing all the old verve, he veered to the right past one challenge as he entered the box. There remained a wall of defenders in front of him, but then came a blur of dazzling footwork, the like of which has been witnessed only very rarely down all the long years the game has been played. Suddenly plunging to his left, he checked, shaped to shoot while under fierce challenge, then dummied and danced left again before cutting abruptly to his right, each time leaving a would-be marker flat-footed and impotent. Finally, somehow, he squirmed to his left yet again before shooting the ball into the corner of the net from a distance of seven yards. It was an astonishing series of deft manoeuvres, all carried out under severe physical pressure yet accomplished with the grace of a ballet dancer.

In the context of all he had once been, most of his work during the sorry death throes of his career was not worth chronicling in detail. But here George Best had bequeathed one golden memory of an otherwise largely forgettable interlude in North America, one supreme proof that when his muse was with him he could still play the game with sublime, incomparable majesty.

16

IN BRONZE
FOR ETERNITY

16
IN BRONZE
FOR ETERNITY

Unbearably sadly, by the late 1980s George Best was in dire financial straits, and, after Manchester United had refused to grant him a testimonial, the Irish Football Association adopted a more charitable approach

So did the people of Belfast. On a night of teeming rain in August 1988, some 25,000 admirers, the biggest gate at Windsor Park for 20 years, braved the weather to watch two all-star teams engage in a richly entertaining 7-6 exhibition match. Having grown a tad porky in recent times, and not wanting to appear tubby on his big night, George had shed 20 pounds for the match and proved more than acceptably light on his feet, sending his home-town fans into raptures by finding the net with a delicate chip.

It was an evening of glorious nostalgia, but with a practical purpose. The game raised more than £100,000 and the emotional 42-year-old told an interviewer afterwards: 'The people of Belfast have saved me. They have given me the means to sort out my finances, and my life.'

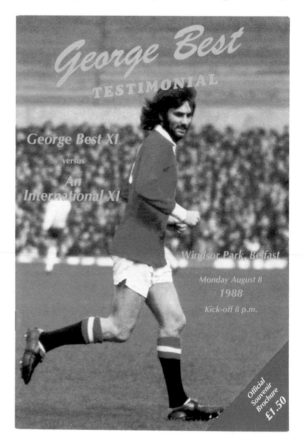

▲ George Best thought the world of Ryan Giggs, both as a player and as a personality. One thing the Irishman envied the Welshman, though, was the way his manager had protected him from the media when he was still an impressionable youngster. However, it would be grossly unfair to hold Sir Matt Busby responsible for Best going off the rails. In hindsight it's easy to discern that George needed more guidance, but at the time there was no precedent in the matter of dealing with pop-idol footballers and Busby did the best he knew how. In contrast, by the time Sir Alex Ferguson knew that Ryan was going to be something special, he knew all about the pitfalls which lay in wait for unwary young superstars, and took the appropriate action. That said, it's clear that George possessed a devilish rebel streak which has not been apparent in Ryan. Let's just say that if Sir Alex

Ferguson had been in charge of George Best, life would have been extremely interesting.

Former Busby Babe John Doherty, a guiding light of the Manchester United Former Players Association and a man sorely missed since he died in 2007, asked and then answered the key question with characteristic wisdom: 'Could the ultimate tragedy of George Best have been avoided if he had been managed differently in the early days? I don't know, but I would doubt it. Even towards the end there was an arrogance about George which proclaimed he was always right, no matter what he did; that he could walk on water; that he was not subject to the normal rules. I'm not sure that Matt Busby, or anybody else, could have been expected to deal with that.'

RYAN GIGGS: *I was lucky enough to spend two days with George Best back in 1993, making a video about the pair of us. The idea was that we visited some of his old haunts and some of mine, as well as places we had in common, like United's training ground at Broughton, The Cliff.*

We met at the Brown Bull in Salford, one of his favourites. He turned out to be a decent pool player, which didn't surprise me, but I won the game. Okay, it was on a fluke shot, but I definitely won!

George was great company, very sharp, very intelligent. I was only about 19 at the time and a little bit nervous about meeting one of the most famous footballers there had ever been anywhere in the world, not just in Manchester United terms. But he was terrific, very engaging, making me feel at ease straight away with a bit of banter.

I still love to look at the old clips of George in action. It's a shame that more footage wasn't preserved because you tend to get the same goals over and over again. That said, they're not too bad, are they!

When I was only 15 years old and playing for England Schoolboys, I used to be compared to George all the time, but I never felt under pressure because of it. To be honest, it never really registered with me. It probably helped that I never saw him play in the flesh which would have emphasised to me just what an icon he was. If the comparisons had been made when I was older and more knowledgeable about him, then it might have been harder. But as it happened, all I could do was take it as a compliment.

I really enjoyed my time with George, and I still look back on it with pleasure. He wasn't one to offer advice, but he was always telling funny little stories and delivering dry one-liners. We got on so well together. Would I have relished playing in the same United side as George? Just a bit!

CLIFF BUTLER: *I can't say I was a close friend of George Best, or even that I knew him well, but on the several occasions I was lucky enough to meet him, invariably I found him to be a warm, softly spoken, extremely modest man. There was never the slightest hint of self-importance or any attempt to project himself as a big-time personality, and I found that extremely refreshing.*

I used to be Manchester United's official photographer, which gave me the chance to meet, and frame, plenty of very famous people. This occasion ranks with one of the truly great moments I enjoyed during my six years behind the lens.

The picture was taken in the Sir Matt Busby Suite at Old Trafford in 1988 in front of the mural painted by the celebrated artist, Walter Kershaw. When George dropped in it was simply too good an opportunity to miss and he was delighted to pose alongside Walter's evocative handiwork.

Not only that, he asked me to send him a copy of the shot for his own collection, and wrote his address in Chelsea, London, on a slip of paper, which I have kept to this very day.

George Best, please meet . . . George Best.

George was the greatest footballer the world has ever seen – that is my humble opinion and it isn't easy for me to say it because Denis Law was far and away my favourite player.

I swear George didn't have a single weakness as a performer. His brilliance and fame sometimes attracted the wrong type of attention from opposition defenders, but he was rarely fazed by the ruthless treatment meted out. There were none of the histrionics we see from today's stars after they have been challenged strongly or fouled.

I doubt that we will ever see George Best's like again and I count myself as enormously privileged to have witnessed most of his incomparable contribution to football's rich and varied history.

◄ Old Trafford bore witness to a breathtaking, deeply emotional scene before Manchester United's first home game following the death of George Best in November 2005. The ground where he will always be revered became a sea of red-shirted images of George shortly before kick-off of a League Cup encounter with West Bromwich Albion, by remarkable coincidence the opponents against whom he made his senior debut for United a little more than 42 years earlier. There was an achingly emotional tribute from his old comrade Sir Bobby Charlton, and surviving members of the Albion side from 14 September 1963 were there to pay their respects.

In offering a typically eloquent summing up to this writer not long before the Irishman's demise, John Doherty sought to deal with what he described as a widespread misconception about George: 'It should be understood clearly that when he finished, he owed nothing to Manchester United. There can be no doubt that they had more than their money's worth out of him. Even if judged purely by bald statistics, his contribution was exceptional, but mere figures don't even begin to describe the pure joy he inspired in those who watched him weaving his magic.

'You never talked about George in terms of a specific position. He might have worn a number seven, or a number eleven sometimes, but he could not be described merely as a winger. He just went out and played, roaming where the spirit took him and cutting defences to ribbons, pretty much at will. George's ability stands comparison with that of anyone who ever lived and I feel desperately sorry that he was reduced to such dire straits as he had reached by 2005, the year of his death.'

PADDY CRERAND: *Cristiano Ronaldo reminded me of George Best a great deal. Oh, Cristiano was of a different build, standing six feet tall whereas George was like a little*

nipper, but they both had the same incredible balance and they were both fantastic in the air. Then there was their courage – George would have tackled Goliath if he was standing between him and goal. The Portuguese was the nearest I have ever seen to George and nobody else comes to mind. I was disappointed when Cristiano left for the simple reason that I love watching great players. They don't come along every day.

'George was finished at United by the age of 26 so it's fair to say he could have done a lot more. But it's good to look at the positive side. He is very high in United's all-time appearances list, in thirteenth position with nobody about to overhaul him any time soon.

DAVID SADLER: *Much is written about the waste of George's talent in his later playing years; people complain that he didn't play on until he was 36, but I never think about that. I just think of all the fabulous things he did, both for Manchester United and for the wider game. He was the greatest footballer I ever played with or against, and he was a loyal friend.*

◀ It was the equivalent of a state funeral, the type of ceremony usually reserved for monarchs or heads of government. On the cold, stormy morning of 3 December 2005 an estimated 100,000 mourners braved the rain and the wind to line the four-mile route of George Best's cortege from his former home in Burren Way in East Belfast to Stormont, the seat of the Northern Ireland Assembly, where the service took place. Live coverage was broadcast around the world, and afterwards George was buried next to his mother in Roselawn Cemetery on a hill overlooking the city.

Memorials abounded, including the naming of Belfast's main airport after George and the issue by the Ulster Bank of commemorative £5 notes. Members of his family set up the George Best Foundation to promote healthy lifestyles in young people through sport, to support those with alcohol or drug problems and to back medical research into illness associated with alcohol misuse.

Overleaf: here stands George Best, cast in bronze for eternity alongside Denis Law and Bobby Charlton at Old Trafford, opposite an equally imposing image of Sir Matt Busby. As long as there is a Manchester United, the little Irishman will never be forgotten.

THE UNITED TRINITY

BEST LAW CHARLTON

ACKNOWLEDGEMENTS

Pat, Rosie and Joe Ponting, as always; Sir Bobby Charlton and Denis Law for their warm and insightful forewords; Rhea Halford for her serene professionalism in charge of the project; Jo Whitford for her endless resourcefulness, expertise and good cheer as the editor; Nick Venables for designing the book.

From the football community: Gordon Banks, Cliff Butler, George Cohen, Paddy Crerand, Jack Crompton, Tony Dunne, Bill Foulkes, Ryan Giggs, Harry Gregg, David Herd, Pat Jennings, Wilf McGuinness, David Meek, Bobby Noble, Frankie Prince, David Sadler, Nobby Stiles, Mike Summerbee, Graham Williams.

Photographic: Andy Cowie and all at Colorsport, Alan Pinnock and Louisa Nolan at the Daily Mail, David Scripps and Vito Inglese at the Daily Mirror, Hayley Newman at Getty Images, Mark Leech at Offside, Lucie Gregory and Jane Speed at the Press Association; Billy Robertson at Action Images.

Also Kerr MacRae of Simon and Schuster; Jack Rollin for his phenomenal knowledge, Chris Welch and Les Gold for their advice and support.

PICTURE CREDITS